May the
be your stre
Nehemi

Barbara Scott

F R O M

RUBBLE

to

RESTORATION

Barbara L. Scott

VMI PUBLISHERS

Partnering With Christian Authors, Publishing Christian and Inspirational Books

Sisters, OR

VMI PUBLISHERS

Partnering With Christian Authors, Publishing Christian and Inspirational Books

a division of VMI Publishers

Sisters, Oregon

www.vmipublishers.com

ISBN: 9781933204307

Library of Congress Control Number: 2006936593

Author Contact: Barbara_L_Scott@Yahoo.com

Printed in the United States of America

Cover design by Joe Bailen

CONTENTS

"There are times when there seems to be a stone wall in front of us, as black as midnight, and there is nothing left but confidence in God. There is no feeling. What you must do is to have a fidelity and confidence to believe that He will not fail, cannot fail."

SMITH WIGGLESWORTH

ACKNOWLEDGEMENTS

Thank you Gary for being my loving companion and strong support for over 33 years. With your strong faith you held my hand during many crises, sat by my hospital bed after surgeries and held me close to your heart through it all.

Thank you dear family, Justin, Nathan and Bethany for contributing to the spiritual fabric of our family. I am blessed beyond measure for the joy of knowing each one of you.

Thank you Brock and Bodie Thoene for your Writers' Workshop, which challenged me to write my own book.

Thank you to the writers' group at YWAM's University of the Nations for your weekly critiques, for your prayers and for your loving encouragement. You have been my cheerleaders for the last two years as we worked hard through laughter and tears. This group was always the highlight of my week.

Thank you Bob Fitts, Jr. for listening to God and giving me a word during the middle of one of your concerts and for inviting us to spend time in Kona at the University of the Nations seeking healing at the feet of Jesus. It changed our lives.

Thank you, Scott and Sandi Tompkins not only for leading the writer's group, and editing my book, but also for your love and friendship.

Above all, I give thanks to my Lord God, the Great Author, who helped me tell this story. May it give hope and inspiration to other families in times of crisis.

INTRODUCTION

The wall of Jerusalem is broken down,
and its gates have been burned with fire.

NEHEMIAH 1:3

It took just 52 days for Old Testament hero, Nehemiah, to rebuild the broken-down wall surrounding Jerusalem. When all seemed lost and impossible, our broken family was rebuilt in a single day! I wouldn't have chosen God's method of restoring our family, but looking back, I wouldn't have it any other way.

July 23, 1998, was the day we had set to blow our family apart, each to go in four separate directions. My husband Gary and I had given up on our marriage, and we were going to get a divorce as soon as our house was sold. Our two sons, Justin, 22 and Nathan, 18, were being kicked out. Watching my family dissolve was devastating, but the task of rebuilding trust and relationship was overwhelming to me. Giving up seemed easier than working to stay together.

Our descent into despair began with a string of devastating medical crises, and escalated with the deaths of my parents and our sons' growing rebellion. Out of shame and fear I hid the boys' drug and alcohol abuse from Gary. That wasn't hard. His career consumed him so much that I hardly knew the man I married. The long hours and travel took Gary away from the family when we needed him most. I became so depressed that I lacked motivation to meet the most basic demands of daily life.

Like Jerusalem, after being defeated by the Babylonians in 539 B.C., our family crumbled. Stone by stone we fell until all that was left was a heap of rubble, which piled so high it was impossible to see the top.

My deception and the rebellion of our sons so devastated Gary that he felt divorce and dissolving the family was the only solution. Distorted truth tore down trust. When the walls caved in I finally turned to the only One I knew who could help us. As the deadline approached, I prayed: "O God, losing my family will destroy me. Please do what ever it takes to put us back together."

God allowed another crisis, the worst we had been through, to set us on a course of healing and reconciliation. During that painful season I was led to study the books of Ezekiel, Haggai, Nehemiah and Ezra, which tell about how the Israelites rebuilt Jerusalem after it had laid in ruins for many years. I became inspired. These great men of God felt called to rebuild Jerusalem and the wall surrounding it. Stone by stone the great fortress was rebuilt. With dedication and determination we, too, could rebuild our family.

It took courage and teamwork, but God used each family member in a unique way to accomplish His purposes.

I want to offer hope to other families who might be experiencing such pain or tragedy. This is the story of our family's terrible undoing and divinely orchestrated reconstruction.

CHAPTER ONE

A DIVINE APPOINTMENT

Do not forget to entertain strangers, for by so doing some people
have entertained angels without knowing it.

HEBREWS 13:2

What does an angel look like? Can they look just like us? I believe Gary and I encountered an angel. Unabashedly, she walked into our lives one Sunday in 1974.

It was a clear, spring morning, and I was loading my saddle and tack in our van. As I stood daydreaming about riding my Arabian mare, Taranna through the wooded hills, I was startled when a family suddenly appeared in front of me.

"Hi, my name is Bobbie," said the young woman with silky, waist-length, black hair. "This is my husband, and our two children."

"Hi," I said as I looked up. "You must be the new family across the street."

I had seen them many times as they walked to church near our home in Eugene, Oregon. A vacant lot with dry, brown grass separated our house from a Pentecostal church, called Faith Center, whose parishioners appeared to mostly be hippies. In the early 1970s we heard that these people were "Jesus freaks."

The couple had a beautiful little girl about three years old and an infant son who was in his father's arms. Bobbie's husband was a tall, handsome blond man. It seemed to me he glowed. I shook my head. *It must be the way the sunlight is catching his hair*, I thought.

"You must have horses. I love riding," Bobbie said.

"I'd love to have you join me. Want to go tomorrow night? The ranch has lots of horses, and I'm sure the owner would let you ride one."

"It will be fun," she said, happily.

Bobbie agreed to come over after dinner the next evening. I was looking forward to having a new friend to go horseback riding with.

After we spoke, I watched them walk across the field and into the old school, which served as the church.

The next evening as we drove 30 minutes to the ranch where I boarded my horse, Bobbie smiled and sang praise songs: "This is the day, this is the day, that the Lord has made, that the Lord has made…"

She seems so happy, I thought. I envied her inner warmth and joy. Why couldn't I be like that?

When we arrived at the Arabian horse ranch, the owner greeted us with a gruff voice. He was a tall, thin, old Native American man who usually had alcohol on his breath and a cigarette hanging from his mouth. He swore at the horses in Chippewa and they obeyed his stern voice. I, too, feared the profane outbursts of this weathered, old horseman, but respected his knowledge and command of horses. He took pride in his prize horses and trophies and immediately started showing them off to my new friend.

As I walked down the aisle between the horse stalls I inhaled deeply. I loved the smell of the horses, the fresh hay, and the wood shavings they spread on the floor of the paddocks. Taranna's ears perked up the moment she heard me whistle our familiar greeting. She poked her head out of the stall and whinnied.

My mare was a stunning cocoa palomino with a flaxen mane and tail that flew in the wind as she cantered. Bobbie borrowed a chestnut-colored gelding. He arched his neck proudly while carrying her around the arena. Bobbie preferred riding bareback and seemed to float as if she were sitting on a cloud. I wasn't sure if she was enjoying herself though. She became quiet and thoughtful.

After riding we brushed the horses down as steam rose from their warm bodies. We covered them with wool-lined canvas blankets and put them back in their stalls.

When we were finished I bantered with the ranch owner and another trainer but Bobbie was still quiet.

"What's wrong?" I asked as we got in the van and began our drive back to town.

"I am not of this world. It makes me sad when I'm around people who are so worldly," she said softly.

"What do you mean?" I had no idea what she was talking about.

"God does not value things of this world. The world idolizes fame, power and riches. God admires humility, submission and gentleness."

Just then an ambulance passed us with its sirens blaring. Bobbie prayed out loud for the person in the ambulance who, no doubt, was ill or injured and his or her family.

"What's up with you anyhow? There's something about you I can't quite understand. You're always singing or praying."

I had set myself up. Bobbie was now able to talk about God, and I was trapped in the van with her for the next 30 minutes as we drove back to town.

"I have Jesus in my heart."

"I'm a Christian too, but you seem different." I was confused.

"You can't experience the joy of the Lord, because you don't know Him."

"How can you say that? You don't even know me," I said, indignantly. "I've gone to church all my life."

"But you don't have a personal relationship with Jesus."

"How do you know?"

"I can tell by your lifestyle," she said and then resumed humming softly.

We didn't talk for quite awhile. It was dark in the van so Bobbie couldn't see me frown. *Why did it seem as if she knew me?*

I had never made the connection between what I believed and how I acted. After graduating from high school I met Gary - a clean-cut guy with short, blond hair and a tall, athletic-looking body. Gary was in his second year of college and said that after graduation he planned to attend seminary and become a pastor. I had never dated such a nice person. The more I got to know him the more I admired his integrity and ambition. We became serious and were married three years later, shortly after Gary graduated from college.

The things Bobbie was saying upset me.

Indignantly I said, "My husband graduated from California Lutheran University where he studied philosophy and religion. We've both been raised in the Church. We were baptized as babies. I went to an all-girls' parochial high school where I attended chapel every day and studied religion classes. Gary and I have both believed in God all of our lives."

She quoted Matthew 7:21, "Not everyone who says to me, 'Lord, Lord,' will enter the kingdom of heaven, but only he who does the will of my Father who is in heaven."

"My husband reads his Bible," I said defensively, my voice rising.

"Wisdom is of God, or wisdom is of the world. 1 Corinthians 3:19 says: 'For the wisdom of this world is foolishness in God's sight,'" she said as she kept smiling.

I began to fume.

Bobbie always answered with a scripture. This lady knows her Bible. How can I argue with that? I'll take her in when we get home, I schemed. *Gary will straighten her out.*

I silently reviewed my lifestyle. *We weren't bad people, but we weren't particularly spiritual either. After Gary decided he wasn't ready to take on the responsibilities of a pastor, he began a career in banking and worked his way up the corporate ladder. He accepted a position with a bank in Eugene, which enabled us to buy our home. I was working as secretary to the manager of another bank. On weekends, we rode horses for recreation or partied with old college buddies and new bank friends. These backyard barbecues always included lots of beer. We had done a little church-hopping, but hadn't found one that was comfortable for us. We hadn't tried the church just across the vacant lot*

When we arrived home I invited Bobbie in and told Gary about our conversation. He immediately became defensive, and the debate was on. We got angry, but Bobbie stayed calm, continuing to quote scripture and speak about God as if she knew Him personally.

Bobbie had wisdom I had never experienced. "You can know about God, but you must take that knowledge and apply it to your lives. Then act according to His character. If you have Godly wisdom it will show in your actions. Human intellect, feelings and emotions must be put aside because it's easy to be seduced by the world's values. Don't adopt worldly ways or justify them. Reject worldly ways. Worldliness is not the way of God. God would urge you to open your eyes to what is right and wrong and then choose to be obedient. Humility and submission need to be part of your daily life."

I told Bobbie it was time for her to leave.

I opened the front door. "Well, if you think I don't have a personal relationship with Jesus, what does it take?" I asked sarcastically.

"Just ask Him into your heart and He'll take care of the rest. I John 2:17 says 'The world and its desires pass away, but the man who does the will of God lives forever.'" She smiled sweetly as she stepped off our porch. I watched her walk across the street to her home.

Gary put on stereo earphones and grabbed his Bible. I was so upset I went to bed. As I lay in the dark recalling all Bobbie had said, troubled thoughts wouldn't allow me to sleep.

Prayer hadn't been part of my life except for memorized prayers before meals and the Lord's Prayer said in unison at church. I didn't know how to begin.

"Jesus, I don't really know what to say, but if you're not in my heart, please come and do whatever you need to do," I prayed softly. Peace fell over me as I drifted off to sleep.

The next Sunday I said, "Gary, I'd like to walk over to that church and see what's going on there."

He agreed to join me.

We decided to sit at the back in case we needed an easy escape. There were about 200 people there from all walks of life. The old building used to be a school and the gymnasium now served as the sanctuary. It still smelled a little like a gym. Basketball hoops were up at each end and ragged curtains hung unevenly over the small windows. The congregation sat on hard, cold folding chairs.

"This doesn't look like any church I've ever been in," I whispered.

We looked for Bobbie and her family, but they weren't there.

As praise music began Gary and I watched in amazement. We had never seen people lift their hands and sing with their eyes closed. People hugged during a greeting time and held hands when they prayed. Gary and I looked at each other and shared a nervous giggle born of ignorance.

Mom had warned me to stay away from fanatics, I reflected while looking around. *I wonder if they roll on the floor?*

As the worship continued we began to feel God's presence.

"They seem very sincere," Gary whispered.

When the pastor spoke, it was the first time either one of us heard a sermon on how to apply the Bible to our daily lives. We knew we were hearing the Truth. Roy Hicks, Jr. taught that God's word is a way of life - seven days a week.

Gary and I began attending Faith Center weekly and God changed our lives. Soon we were worshipping and praising God with the rest of the congregation. We rededicated our lives and together began seeking Him. Some of our old habits began to fall away. Our old friends stopped inviting us to their parties, but we gained new Christian friends.

Bobbie had planted seeds within my spirit. I saw an inner beauty in her, and it created a spiritual hunger within me. She had ministered to my empty soul when the shallowness of my faith was revealed.

How could I tell Bobbie what it meant to me that she was bold enough to challenge me to a deeper walk with the Lord? Our lives were touched, and I wanted to thank her. An apology was needed for the rude and inconsiderate way I had treated her. But we never saw Bobbie or her family at church. When we asked the head usher, pastors and Bible study leaders about this family, no one had ever seen them or heard of them. How could that be? Bobbie and her family passed our house three to four times a week for months on their way to that church.

Gary and I walked across the street and knocked on their front door. The house was vacant. We never saw them move out, nor did any of our neighbors, and we never saw them again.

God brought Bobbie into our lives to bring us a message that He wanted to have a personal relationship with us.

CHAPTER TWO

THE JOY OF THE LORD

The joy of the Lord is your strength.

NEHEMIAH 8:10

Gary and I had attended church all of our lives, but at Faith Center Foursquare Church we were learning how to have a living, every-day relationship with our Lord. We knew most of the Bible stories. Now we were learning how to apply the whole of God's Word to our lives.

In 1975 Faith Center bought our little house and the vacant lot next to it to expand the church. We also were expanding. We bought ten acres of open land west of Eugene. Our "ranch" had a pasture for horses and cows, a large vegetable garden, a chicken coop, and a place for cats and dogs. We had a modular home built on a small rise overlooking our spread. It seemed an ideal place for raising children.

Our first child, Justin. arrived in 1976, followed by Nathan in 1980. What incredible gifts from God were these two precious, healthy sons! And if that weren't enough blessing, Gary had achieved the status of bank vice president before he turned 30. During those busy years I took care of the boys, showed horses and also worked part-time for another bank.

It soon became obvious that our sons were both fearless and very competitive. Justin began BMX (bicycle motocross) racing when he was seven and was soon sponsored by a bike factory in California. A natural athlete, Justin and his bike became one as they flowed around turns and flew over jumps. He ranked #1 in the state of Oregon for his age group when he was eight and was nationally ranked by nine years old.

Not to be outdone, Nathan believed he could do anything Justin did despite a four-year age difference. He started riding a two-wheel bicycle when he was three and began BMX racing when he was only four! During the years the boys raced bikes we followed the BMX racing circuit through Washington, Oregon, California and Nevada.

In 1984 when Gary accepted a position with Seafirst Bank in Seattle, Washington we moved to Bellevue, a suburb on the east side. The Snoqualmie Pass ski resort was only a 45-minute drive from our home, so we began skiing when the boys were young. Gary loved the sport, and his skills earned him a spot on the National Ski Patrol. Justin and Nathan channeled the same reckless passion they had for biking into downhill skiing. All four of us loved spending weekends together barreling down the majestic Cascade Mountains. We often marveled at the white splendor God placed all around us, and it seemed like life couldn't get much better.

I still had many questions concerning my faith and to gain a deeper understanding of the Bible, I enrolled in a five-year course with an inter-denominational organization called Bible Study Fellowship. A Christian friend, who worked with me at the bank, also enrolled in the study. She and I spent a lot of time talking about the Lord and issues that came up in the Bible study. I told her I had two major roadblocks in my faith.

"I love my husband and the boys so much I can't stand the thought of losing any one of them. If one of them died I don't know if my faith could withstand the pain. Would I still believe in God or would I blame Him? Also, I'm not sure if prayer really works. I know it helps us. But, is it just a positive mental exercise or does God really hear us? Does it change anything if He does?"

My friend said, "I'm sure God will reveal the answers to those questions if you continue to seek Him."

Another troubling question came from reading I Corinthians 3:13, which says, *"There is going to come a time of testing at Christ's Judgment Day to see what kind of material each builder has used. Everyone's work will be put through the fire so that all can see whether or not it keeps its value and what was really accomplished."*

Was that scripture meant for today or just on Judgment Day? Did God put us through trials to strengthen us or to see if our faith would remain strong? For the next few years I would still be pondering those questions, but a time was coming when I would know the answers.

In 1986, Gary was hired by Eastside Foursquare Church in Kirkland, WA, to be its Chief Financial Officer. The church had grown from a congregation of about 200 people in 1984 to 4,000 in 1986. Pastor Doug Murren had to hold five services every Sunday. Gary's job involved the financing to purchase land and build a new building. We also were the coordinators for five cell groups, and I led a women's Bible study group. Gary 's upbringing in a Christian home, his education at California Lutheran University, and our experience at Faith Center gave him a foundation upon which his faith now soared.

Life seemed incredibly good until a series of serious medical problems began to plague our family in 1987. That September I had a hip replacement to correct congenital hip dysplasia that had caused me years of pain. Because of complications, it was followed with another surgery to the same leg in October and another the following October.

In December of 1988, my doctor said my hip was sufficiently healed and gave me permission to ski. Before the surgeries I had been a good skier, and I longed to be outside with the family. He said if I took easy ski runs I should be okay.

"Just slide gently down the bunny slopes," the doctor warned.

I thought I'd finally be able to live a normal life. In a ski movie I'd seen a guy with two artificial hips swishing down the slopes in waist deep powder. So why not me? I wanted so much to get back to this treasured family activity.

The first time we all went skiing again was exhilarating. The crisp winter air, the beauty of the mountains, and the excitement of my family were a feast for my senses. Gary was an amazing skier - always working on his form. Justin made skiing look effortless. His ankles and knees seemed to be glued together. All he had to do was swivel his hips, and it looked like he was dancing down the mountain. Eight-year-old Nathan plunged down every ski run with reckless abandon - his jacket unzipped and flapping in the wind behind him like wings.

On Christmas Day we were surprised by how listless Nathan was. "I have a tummy ache," he whined. We dismissed it as Christmas excitement and too much candy. But in the early afternoon after all the relatives arrived, he continued to complain and seemed indifferent to the smells of turkey, pies and homemade dinner rolls flooding the room. At Christmas dinner, Nathan wouldn't touch a bite. He went to his bedroom and lay on his bed.

It wasn't like my happy-go-lucky, active little boy to not eat or not play with his Christmas toys. Late in the afternoon one of the older cousins tried to tickle Nathan hoping to cheer him up. Nathan's screams sent us rushing to the room. Something was very wrong.

Gary scooped Nathan up as gently as possible, and we rushed him to the hospital.

"He has acute appendicitis and needs emergency surgery," the ER doctor told us.

Nathan began to cry. I tucked the new stuffed dinosaur, "Littlefoot," under his arm. "Littlefoot will stay with you. Mom and Dad will be waiting right here and praying for you." I kissed him softly on the cheek and played with his curly, blond hair until they wheeled him away.

Two hours later, the surgeon came into the waiting room smiling, "We caught Nathan's appendix just before it ruptured. He shouldn't ski for about three weeks, but soon he will be as good as new."

On New Year's Eve two other families from our church gathered with us in our home. It was our tradition to "pray in the New Year" with our closest friends. Snuggled in front of our warm fireplace we went around the room recounting things we were most grateful for during the past year and stating our New Year's resolution. I was thankful that Nathan was on the mend and my hip was healed so well that I was able to ski again. My New Year's resolution for 1989 would be to seek the joy of the Lord - not happiness, but the kind of God-inspired joy, which glows from the inside out. I had seen that depth of joy in only a few people. One was Bobbie, the woman we believe was an angel. I wanted a joy that rises above circumstances to focus on the character of God. The verse I chose for the year was Psalm 66:1, "Shout with joy to God, all the earth!"

On January 7th after spending the day inside the ski patrol building taking care of Nathan, who was still recovering from his surgery, I begged Gary to stay and night-ski with me. "You, Justin and I could just take a few runs and then we'll all go home." Gary said it was icy, but after I begged some more, he consented. Another ski patroller agreed to stay with Nathan while we made a few runs.

It was a cold night and the moon made a path across the snow as we rode the chair lift to the top of the mountain. I inhaled the crisp fresh air. Night skiing was so quiet all you could hear was the squeak of the chair lift and an occasional gleeful laugh of a skier in the distance. I smiled as I watched Justin gracefully ski down the hill then stop to wait for us. He made skiing look so easy. Gary was next. About half way down he stopped and shouted up to me, "There's an icy patch down here. Be careful!"

I was nervous as I started skiing down the hill. Hadn't the doctor told me to stay on the bunny slopes? Here I was up on an advanced run with hard, icy snow. As I came slowly down the hill I hit the ice and couldn't turn. My body fell to the right in an effort not to fall on my bad left hip. But, my left leg wasn't strong enough to turn and it went the other way. I felt an explosion of pain as I twisted and hit the ground.

Gary sent Justin to summon ski patrollers. "Tell them it's a broken femur. They need to bring a toboggan and a Hare splint traction device."

Justin bolted off like a rifle shot. On his way, he spotted some ski patrollers on the chair lift and shouted the instructions up to them. He then raced down to where other ski patrollers could radio for help. Soon I was surrounded with friends who knew what they were doing.

"Mom... broke... her leg," Justin gasped out of breath, as he burst into the ski patrol lodge.

Nathan panicked. Without a coat, hat or gloves he dashed from the building and began running up the mountain. Thankfully, a patroller on a ski mobile spotted him. He scooped up Nathan, gave him his coat and hat and together they raced up the mountain to the accident scene. They arrived just as I was being transferred to the toboggan.

On the long, slow descent I felt every bump. The most painful part was when the patrollers had to take my ski boot off. They gave me Demerol to ease the pain, but I really squeezed a friend's hand as they pulled off my boot.

Paramedics arrived to take me to the hospital. As they were loading me into the ambulance Nathan was crying and grabbed my hand. "Don't forget, Mom, your New Year's resolution for this year is the joy of the Lord."

Out of the mouths of babes, I thought, choking back a tear. It was just one week since I had made that New Year's resolution. It gave me something to think about during the trip to the hospital.

Doctors diagnosed it as a spiral fracture from just above my knee about six inches up my thigh.

I was put in traction for three days before they could do surgery. Due to having a hip prosthesis I couldn't have the normal procedure of a rod down my leg. A steel plate was placed along the femur with nine screws to hold it in place. Ten days in the hospital and eight months in a plastic cast with crutches would give me a lot of time to wonder why God had allowed so many bad things to happen to our family in such a short time.

Several years later, I was organizing books and among my collection found *Joy That Lasts*, by Gary Smalley. On the inside cover was a message from my husband: "To my loving wife, A happy theme for 1989. I love you."

I could not have imagined how severely my resolution to have joy would be tested in 1989 and the years that followed. Choosing joy is a decision. To choose joy, despite the circumstances we faced, would be an extremely difficult challenge.

CHAPTER THREE

THE HARDEST RACE

Therefore, since we are surrounded by such a great cloud of witnesses,
let us throw off everything that hinders and the sin that so easily entangles,
and let us run with perseverance the race marked out for us.

HEBREWS 12:1

March 10, 1989, began like most Fridays during ski season. We packed up our green Plymouth Valiant with a chest full of food, sleeping bags, duffel bags, ski boots and poles. On the roof rack were three sets of skis. Once loaded, we headed for the Snoqualmie Pass ski resort east of Seattle, where we could stay in the ski patrol dorms. On crutches and my leg in a cast, I wouldn't be doing any skiing, but I enjoyed the camaraderie of other ski patrol families.

Gary's career was in banking but skiing was his passion. He looked as professional in his ski patrol uniform as he did in his banker's three-piece suit. The boys talked about how "cool" it was that their dad was a "real" ski patroller. All three headed out skiing as soon as they could get on their gear. At the end of that deliciously pleasant evening the boys came bursting into the ski patrol building with tales of their latest adventures—new trails discovered and new tricks performed. Justin and Nathan were convinced they were "totally awesome" skiers and would grow up to be on the US Olympic ski team.

Saturday morning we awoke to a warm drizzle. The boys groaned about bad snow conditions during breakfast. Justin was now on the downhill racing team and had a race later that day. Ever confident, he told us, "If I could race my bike in the rain and mud, I know I can 'blow them all away' today."

I watched the morning races from under the shelter of a tarp. Gary and Nathan joined me to watch Justin's run. His team came down last. Although Justin did well, he was obviously unhappy with his time and the rainy conditions. Race officials were awarding participant ribbons to some and telling other racers to return for the finals after lunch. Justin would be back for the finals.

The sun broke through the clouds just as we scattered for lunch. The rain and the 42-degree weather left snow piled up in soggy, wet heaps like snow cones. These slushy conditions made the ski runs slow and the turns particularly difficult.

Justin gulped down his lunch so he could return to the racecourse. He wanted to do a few practice runs before the finals of that afternoon's giant slalom race. He was in a grumpy mood so I let him go. (If only I had made him stay with us a little longer…)

"What's air-evac?" I asked Gary, as I finished putting the remainders of our lunch in the cooler.

"Air-evacuation," he said.

Moments earlier patrol radios echoed with news that there had been an accident and a backboard was needed.

The usually bustling lunch-room suddenly fell silent as ski patrollers and their families listened to the radio calls. Soon there was another one confirming the need for Airlift Northwest.

Gary looked grave. "We expected some accidents today because of the slushy snow conditions, but this sounds bad."

Gary hurried off to the first aid room to prepare for the patient. I quickly followed, my heart pounding. The director of the ski school and another ski patroller met us at the door. Something about their solemn expressions told me this was really serious.

The muscles in the Director's jaw twitched as he tried to speak. He took a deep breath and leaned against a table for support.

"It's Justin. He's got a serious head injury."

"No," I screamed, wrapping my arms around my stomach as if to hold myself together.

"Are you sure it's Justin?" gasped Gary.

They both nodded gravely. Our son had missed a turn and slammed into something up there on the mountain.

"How bad is it?" croaked Gary, barely able to speak

"He's unconscious and bleeding from the head."

A wave of fear and nausea surged through me. "Lord, have mercy on my son," I wailed, my body wracked with sobs.

As patrollers and their families began to pour into the room I continued to scream, "No! No! No-o-o!" Many gave me hugs but there was no comfort in that moment. Nathan heard my screams and ran to me with a terrified look in his big, brown eyes. He flung his arms around my waist and clung to me.

I didn't know how to comfort him. How could I tell him his brother was traumatically injured? All I could do was to hug him tight and whisper, "Keep praying for Justin."

"God, save Justin." I prayed over and over, not caring who might hear me.

"I'm going up there," Gary said, as he grabbed his skis and flew out the door.

I stood in the doorway shaking as a crowd gathered about 200 yards up the mountain. The crowd looked like a sea of rust-colored jackets with blue yolks and big gold crosses on their backs, the uniform

of the National Ski Patrol. Within a few minutes whistle blasts signaled
that they were bringing our son down in a toboggan.

"Clear the way," someone shouted. "Toboggan coming through."
More shrill whistle blasts. I noticed Gary skiing alongside the toboggan. They were in front of me within seconds.

I gasped when I saw Justin. He was gray and groaning with every
labored breath. His eyes were closed.

Above the noise of the crowd, I yelled, "Justin, this is Mom. Please
answer me." He just lay there in his new ski outfit, unable to respond.

Uniformed medics from Airlift Northwest were already there. An
IV was started and tests were performed to see if Justin would respond
to pain. When his eyes were checked they were diverted to the left.

"That's an indication of severe bleeding and pressure in Justin's
brain," we were informed.

The paramedics told us there wasn't room in the helicopter for
family members. They needed all available space to concentrate on
keeping Justin alive. The backboard was swiftly loaded into the helicopter.

Gary and I stood in the parking lot supporting each other as we
watched the helicopter, carrying our precious son, disappear over the
mountains into the gray sky.

That hour-long drive to the Seattle hospital was the longest drive
of our lives. We alternately cried, prayed and encouraged each other.

I agonized about something I'd said earlier. I told Gary about a talk
I had with my friend from church.

"I told her that even though I've believed in God for many years,
I don't know if my faith can withstand the loss of you, Justin or
Nathan. Could this be my fault for doubting God?" I asked wiping
away tears. Filled with emotion Gary reached over and stroked my
hand. Only God could give me the answers I sought.

As we rounded the junction from I-90 to I-5, Harborview
Hospital came into view, sitting on a hill above Seattle like a lion protecting its domain.

The three of us went directly to the Emergency Room, still dressed in our ski clothes. Nurses met us at the door.

"Justin has not regained consciousness," we were told. "He has been intubated and rushed in for a CT scan." I didn't understand the significance when we were ushered past the busy waiting room and shown to a plush, comfortable private waiting room.

Why were we receiving special treatment? I wondered. I later learned that the private waiting room is reserved for families of patients in critical condition.

My sister, brother-in-law, our Associate Pastor, and a friend from church arrived. As we waited, we joined together in prayer.

Gary and I recounted what others told us about the accident. An instructor had been watching as Justin was making his practice run through the gates. He missed one of the turns and left the racecourse skiing into the thick, ungroomed snow. The racecourse was set close to an abandoned rope tow-shack. When Justin was unable to turn, he flew headfirst into that old shack, shattering his skull. The shack was built up several feet on pilings and Justin slid under the building amongst other debris, which was the apparent cause of abdominal bleeding.

Every few minutes a uniformed ER nurse would come into the waiting room to update us. Soon a kindly, soft-spoken doctor with white hair and a white beard came in. He introduced himself as Dr. Paul Kanev, a neurosurgeon.

"Justin has multiple skull fractures including a subdural and epidural hematoma and internal abdominal bleeding," said the doctor. When we asked him to interpret, he explained that Justin was bleeding badly on the right front part of his brain and must have brain surgery immediately. They would also open his abdomen to stop the bleeding and check his spleen.

"What are his chances?" I asked trembling, almost holding my breath. Gary and I were holding hands. I was terrified of the answer.

"We don't know yet," answered the neurosurgeon, gravely. "His eyes are diverted to the left side due to the pressure the bleeding has caused on the right side of the brain."

"What does that mean?"

"It's ominous," he replied solemnly.

"Don't let him die," I begged, not sure if I was addressing the doctor or God.

As the evening grew late my sister offered to take Nathan home and keep him overnight.

During Justin's surgery the clock seemed to stand still.

In the last two years our family had been through so much. I had undergone five surgeries on my leg beginning with the hip replacement. Then came Nathan's emergency surgery for appendicitis and my skiing accident. All this was so hard on Nathan. He really fell apart when I broke my femur on the ski slope. How was he going to cope with this? Justin was more than a brother—he was Nathan's best friend.

Gary and I couldn't eat. We couldn't sleep. We paced the hall. We prayed. We cried. We didn't know what to do.

Dr. Kanev and another surgeon finally came into the waiting room and told us Justin was out of surgery. The doctors looked tired and sad. They explained that the epidural hematoma (a blood clot between the skull and the tissue around the brain) had been about the size of a sand dollar. The subdural hematoma (inside the brain) was only the size of a dime but was more dangerous because of its location.

"We know this is devastating. It's hard on us, too. It's especially hard when it's a child," the doctor said.

"Tomorrow is Sunday," said his assistant. "I'll be in church praying for Justin and your family." It was reassuring to know one of Justin's doctors was a Christian.

When we finally were allowed into the Intensive Care Unit, the charge nurse tried to educate us, but nothing would prepare us for what we would see. Justin had a "bolt" (inner cranial device) in his head hooked to a monitor to measure the pressure in his brain. He was unable to breathe on his own so he was on a respirator. Wires and IV's were in every limb and in his chest. Justin's chest rose and fell with the rhythm of the respirator as it whooshed and released. Restraints tied around Justin's wrists, ankles and chest kept him from disconnecting any tubes when he became agitated.

We didn't know if Justin could hear us, but between sobs I whispered, "We love you so much. Mom and Dad are here with you. Many people are praying for you."

A recliner chair was placed next to his bed. We took turns trying to rest. Every time Gary dozed off he would groan from deep in his soul making animal-like sounds. Then he would wake himself up with a jerk and bolt upright, gasping for air.

I finally slept for a few hours. It was still dark outside when I slowly entered that twilight sleep just before becoming fully awake. My thoughts were a jumble and I tried to convince myself that this had all just been a bad dream. Then I remembered this was a real-life nightmare. "God, please heal Justin," I prayed as I opened my eyes to face the day.

With stethoscopes around their necks and clipboards in their hands, a team of doctors burst in at 7 a.m., as they would every morning thereafter. General surgeons and residents accompanied the Chief of Neurology. They performed tests on Justin and tried to get him to react by raising a finger or squeezing a hand.

The neurologist explained that they expected Justin to be in a coma for a week to ten days. He told us how impressed they were with the ski patrollers' quick decision to call for a helicopter. We had originally thought Justin should be transported to Children's Hospital, but the ski patrollers insisted he must go to Harborview. That decision also was divinely orchestrated. The neurosurgical team was not in another surgery—they were available when Justin arrived.

"Justin only had thirty minutes to spare," the neurosurgeon informed us.

Events had to take place exactly as they did to save Justin's life.

"Will he be normal again?" I asked every time the doctors came into ICU.

"We can't tell yet."

After several days of asking the same question the neurosurgeon took us aside and asked a question that completely changed my perspective and my attitude.

"Can you love your son just the way he is?"

Of course, the answer was, "Yes." We would love our son no matter what.

"Justin may be exactly as you see him for the rest of his life. Any improvement beyond what you see will be a bonus."

Reality set in. We were in this for the long haul.

We spent many hours, day and night, sitting by Justin's bed watching for any sign of consciousness.

Life without Justin seemed unimaginable. I just wanted him to live, but talking with the doctor changed my outlook.

That day as I watched Justin struggle for life, I found a Bible in the nightstand and began to read the book of John. I realized God had a son He loved even more than I loved Justin. He had watched His son suffer and die.

"God," I cried out in prayer, "I'm sorry for hanging on too tightly to the gifts you have given me. Thank you for 12 wonderful years with Justin. I don't want to selfishly hang on if he won't have a quality life. I release him back to you, Father. Your will be done."

CHAPTER FOUR

THE VALLEY OF THE
SHADOW OF DEATH

Even though I walk through the valley of the shadow of death,
I will fear no evil, for you are with me.

PSALM 23:4

The bedside vigil continued.

I stroked the cheek of my beautiful boy, as my tears fell on the bed. *Should I be praying for life or death?* I really didn't want Justin to live if that meant being a vegetable for the rest of his life. It was hard to let go though.

Why had this happened? I had so many questions for God. I wished I could have a conversation with Him.

God do you take a personal interest in our prayers? Are you a merciful God? Are You interested in the fate of good people?

It was as if in my heart I heard, "Be strong. Do not fear."

When our associate pastor, Jerry Cook, came to the hospital I talked to him about my questions and he said, "We must give our prayers hands and feet to do what God requires of us."

"I don't think I have the strength to go through this. I feel like I'm going to lose it," I answered.

Pastor Jerry said, "God gives you extra grace in times like this. I know you can get through with His help."

Suddenly, I felt optimistic that God would give me the strength to deal with the future, whatever that might be.

As we sat beside Justin's bed in the ICU Gary and I talked about the things that delighted us most about Justin.

"I liked it when he'd come in our bedroom at night, plop down in our easy chair and say, 'Let's talk.'"

Choking up Gary said, "I enjoyed the intimate, quiet moments we shared riding on the chairlift up the mountain."

We couldn't help but reflect back on Justin's life, character and endearing qualities. At the age of four Justin accepted Jesus as his Lord and Savior. He begged to be baptized when he was six. We thought that maybe he didn't understand what it all meant so we had an elder at church counsel him. She said they didn't usually baptize someone so young but she couldn't hold him back from seeking righteousness.

Justin's competitive spirit came out in all areas of his life. When he was in first grade he won a speech contest and got to participate at the state level. He had been racing BMX (bicycle motocross) bikes beginning at age seven. When he was nine Justin won the Oregon State Governor's Cup race. He went on to place 4th in the Honeycomb Grand Nationals held in Las Vegas. Justin also entered talent shows and even won a Duncan Yo-Yo Championship. He attempted to be the best at whatever he did.

Mr. Lewis, Justin's sixth grade homeroom teacher, told us that our son was the kind of student every teacher loves. "He's so enthusiastic, we put him up front so the rest of the kids can catch his energy."

One day Justin announced that he wanted to become our state's governor. We weren't surprised by this lofty goal. Those who knew

Justin best believed that, with his drive, he would achieve almost any goal. He thought he could do anything, and he had everyone else convinced he was right.

Reminiscing about Justin's drive and enthusiasm for life gave us hope that these characteristics would help him now.

There was a constant stream of people coming to the hospital to support us, pray with us, hold us and bring us food. Friends from church, fellow ski patrollers and relatives all came. Even a few people came who didn't know us. After hearing about the accident on the news or reading about it in the newspaper they wanted to share similar stories and encourage us. My sister took phone calls from Justin's classmates, TV, newspapers and friends.

The outpouring we received from the community amazed us. We were seeing the Church in action. Justin's class at the Middle School had a bake sale to raise funds to help with his medical expenses. The ski patrollers started a trust fund. Nathan's Cub Scout troop had a cake sale. A women's group I belonged to had a garage sale. We heard that many churches and different denominations were praying for our family. Through the prayers of others, I began to feel wrapped in God's love. I sensed that God was in control. God was always with us. We didn't go through any part of this alone.

Friends and relatives helped care for Nathan, and he was brought to the hospital to see Justin every day. Although he was only allowed in ICU a few minutes at a time, he would stand outside the door and hope he could catch a glimpse of his brother as someone came in or out of the door. Eight-year-old Nathan's generous spirit showed when he gave Justin the stuffed dinosaur, Littlefoot, he had received for Christmas.

"Littlefoot was with me when I had my appendix out. Maybe he'll help Justin," Nathan said, tenderly as he placed his beloved stuffed animal in his older brother's arms.

We prayed over Justin and when he seemed the most fitful, we read scriptures to soothe him. We taped a sticky note on the machine above

Justin's head, which measured the pressure in his brain. It read, *"Peace I leave with you; my peace I give to you. I do not give to you as the world gives. Do not let your hearts be troubled and do not be afraid"* (John 14:27).

Many months later we took Justin back to thank the nurses and show him the ICU room where he fought for his life. The sticky note was still taped to the machine above the now empty bed.

It's not like in the movies when the person in a coma suddenly opens their eyes and asks, "What day is this? How long have I been here?"

Recovering from a critical closed-head injury is a slow process. One night Gary stayed with Justin, and I went home in an attempt to get a few hours of sleep. When I walked into Justin's ICU room the next morning Gary was all smiles.

"Justin, who's that?" Gary said, looking at me.

"Mom."

I sat on the edge of his bed and hugged him, crying freely. Justin's arm came up around my neck. What a wonderful feeling to know my son recognized me!

Later that morning day Justin said, "Scissors."

"What do you want scissors for, honey?"

He couldn't tell us, but he began to tug at the restraints. We think he wanted to cut all the tubes and restraints holding him down.

Justin was crying in the afternoon.

"What's the matter, sweetie, does your head hurt?" I asked.

"My wiener!"

Oh, it felt so good to laugh. He just shattered his skull, had brain surgery and abdominal surgery, but his biggest concern was the catheter!

That's my boy.

After one week, Justin's level of consciousness improved and the respirator was removed as well as all the tubes and IVs. He then was moved to Children's Hospital. We were told he would be in rehab two to three months.

One evening as we pushed him around in a wheelchair, Justin caught a glimpse of himself in a mirror.

"Ugly," he said.

He had lost twenty pounds and had dark circles under his eyes.

"No. Beautiful." I said, smiling at the reflection in the mirror.

As Justin was able to understand, we began to explain what had happened and why he was in the hospital.

"Work hard so we can take you home," I encouraged.

His dad put his face close to Justin's and looked him in the eyes. "This is the hardest race you'll ever have to be in, son." Gary had been Justin's BMX coach and knew how to inspire him. "We know, with God's help, you'll win this race. You've always been a winner."

It was like a rebirthing process. Justin had to learn everything all over again. Feeding himself was messy at first. Walking wasn't too bad, but he was especially excited one day when he returned from physical therapy to announce, "I ran today." Speech therapy was frustrating because word retrieval was very difficult. The therapist would show him a picture of an anchor and he would say, "sailor." When he saw a picture of a chimney he said, "smoke."

Yet, we could see his progress daily. Justin was a long way from a full recovery, but we could see glimpses of our old son.

Justin was not about to let this obstacle defeat him. Beating all expectations, he was released from Children's Hospital after 37 days, but had to return as an outpatient every day for the next four months.

With the help of a tutor Justin returned to school the following September, and he continued his race for a full recovery. Justin graduated from high school with the rest of his class and completed two years of college. He had won the biggest race of his life.

The race is not to the swift or the battle to the strong, nor does food come to the wise, or wealth to the brilliant, or favor to the learned; but time and chance happen to them all.

ECCLESIASTES 9:11

I no longer doubted God's ability to sustain me in tragedy. My faith withstood my worst fear; in fact it grew stronger. It was no coincidence that the ski patrollers called for Airlift Northwest immediately, and they were not on another call. Their fastest helicopter was available to transport Justin. It was no coincidence that the decision was made to take Justin to Harborview Hospital, a Level 1 trauma center. The neurological team was not in another operation and was waiting to perform surgery when Justin arrived. God did not intend for Justin to die on a ski slope that day. He had other plans for Justin. God was, is and always will be in control.

Justin Racing

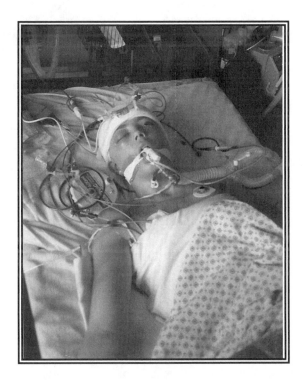

Justin in a coma at
Harbowview Hospital

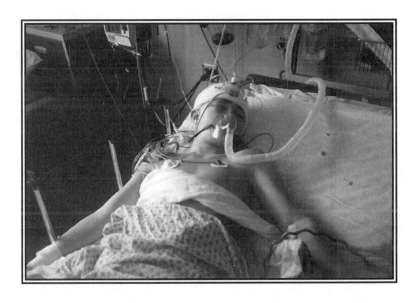

CHAPTER FIVE

ENEMY AT OUR GATES

Be self-controlled and alert. Your enemy the devil prowls around like a
roaring lion looking for someone to devour. Resist him, standing firm in
the faith, because you know that your brothers throughout the world
are undergoing the same kind of sufferings.

1 PETER 5:5-9

In August, 1989, Gary went back to
work for the bank. They made him a regional vice president restoring
his seniority and benefits as if he hadn't been gone for three years. Gary
dove into the new position at the bank, seeking to exceed all goals the
bank set for him. His career flourished.

I thought our family was on the mend, but our medical problems
were not over. One pleasant August evening five months after Justin's
accident I walked into our bedroom, and Gary was writhing in pain on
the floor. He had had a kidney stone ten years earlier so I immediately
recognized the symptoms. But this was no ordinary kidney stone

attack. By the time we got to the hospital Gary's body was going into shock. His heart rate dropped to thirty-three beats per minute. Gary was whisked away and nurses would not let me accompany him into the Emergency Room. They were afraid they were losing him.

Not Gary, Lord! He had been my pillar during our previous crises—a tower of strength during my surgeries; my rock during Nathan's appendectomy; my refuge during Justin's accident. I sometimes looked to Gary for help even more than Jesus. I knew that would have to change, but I counted on my husband in so many ways.

As I sat in the waiting room, I started to assail God. *Hadn't we suffered enough for several lifetimes? Didn't we pass the test?* At the time, I thought that God put each individual or family to the test, and if they passed, then there wouldn't be any more problems. My understanding of all this was weak.

I hadn't realized it, but my Heavenly Father had spent years preparing me. The enemy was at our gates. Now it was time to stand up, practice what I believed and stay focused.

I called our Christian friends, who started a prayer chain. I got out my Bible to recall the promises of God. The Lord showed me His might and ability through Proverbs 18:10 which says, *The name of the Lord is a strong tower, the righteous run to it and are safe.* I also found strength in 2 Samuel 22:2, *The Lord is my rock, my fortress and my deliverer, my God is my rock in whom I take refuge, my shield and the horn of my salvation. He is my stronghold, my refuge and my savior.*

I paraphrased Nehemiah 1:5 and prayed it repeatedly: *O Lord, God of heaven, the great and awesome God, who keeps His covenant of love with those who love Him and obey His commands, let your ear be attentive and your eyes open to hear the prayer your servant is praying before you. I confess my sin of not putting you first in my life and acting very selfishly. You are my first love and I choose to return to seek you above all else.*

The Emergency Room doctors were able to stabilize Gary's heart rate and pull him out of shock. His kidney stone was large and had to be removed surgically. It would be a long recovery, but the danger was past. When Gary got home from the hospital our family spent a lot of time cuddled on our big bed watching movies.

One day Gary told the boys, "Mom and I have been talking. We've decided to get a puppy. Justin can't ski for at least a year. So, maybe the puppy could be trained in 4-H obedience classes. What do you think?"

"Mom, is Dad still on drugs from his surgery?" Nathan asked playfully. Gary had told them many times that a dog was out of the question.

It took a few weeks, but Gary recovered beautifully. We turned the selection of a Brittany puppy into a fun family event. We named our new dog Tucker and he became a much-loved member of our family.

In December, I needed hip surgery again. The doctor wanted me to take iron capsules to build up my blood. Tucker put his paws up on the bathroom counter one morning and ate my bottle of iron tablets. I called the Veterinarian then rushed Tucker to the office. When I arrived she was on the phone to the Poison Control Center. She informed me that Tucker ate five times the amount of iron it would take to kill a human adult. They managed to pump his stomach and save his life.

Two weeks later, on the morning of my hip revision surgery I awoke to a THUD, then glass breaking. I jumped out of bed and glanced at the clock: 4:30 a.m. In that half-awake, confused state I realized it wasn't the alarm. I wasn't due to leave for the hospital for another hour. Suddenly, Nathan was screaming! I ran to the hallway where I found Grandma Scott standing with her hands over her face crying. She had come to take care of the boys while I was in the hospital. I couldn't imagine what had happened. Gary jumped ahead of me to the bathroom, where Nathan sat holding his dying hamster, Henrietta. The blood-spattered bathroom was covered with broken glass, cedar shavings and the remains of the aquarium, which served as Henrietta's cage.

"My hampster was running on her wheel. It was squeaking. I

couldn't sleep," 9-year-old Nathan sobbed, big tears running down his cheeks. "I put her in the bathroom. Dad, do something."

"I needed to wash my hands," cried Grandma. "I put the aquarium on the back of the toilet and when the hamster got on her treadmill it tipped over."

In a compassionate, soft voice Gary said, "Son, there's nothing we can do. Tell Henrietta you love her. She's been a good pet. We'll stay with her until she's at rest."

Sleepy Justin was now stumbling down the hallway, rubbing his eyes. "What's going on?"

Total chaos. I was supposed to leave for the hospital in half an hour for a revision to the prosthesis in my left hip.

Nathan held Henrietta as her life slipped away. Gary sat on the stairs leading to the family room with his arm around his youngest son.

"Let's put her on a beautiful cloth in a shoe box and I'll help you bury her tonight. I've got to take Mom to the hospital now, honey."

Although big for his age, nine-year-old Nathan looked small and sad as he sat in the big, blue easy chair in his red plaid pajamas when I kissed him good-bye.

"Will Mom die, too?"

I knew that Nathan was making a connection between his hamster's death and my surgery. He was hysterical. Nathan was afraid that I would die, too. While Nathan was crying for his pet I had to leave for the hospital.

These crises with the pets demonstrate that our whole household was under attack. The enemy was trying to rob us of joy any way he could.

I got through that surgery, but my prosthetic hip failed again in February of 1993, and again in November of 1993. More reconstructive surgery was necessary.

Friends kept telling us that we were under satanic attack. *What did that mean?* Neither Gary nor I were brought up in Churches that talked much about Satan. *If we are saved,* I wondered, *what are we saved from?*

In 1990 our pastor, Doug Murren, published a book called, *Is it Real When it Doesn't Work?* (Thomas Nelson Publishers) He wrote about us in chapter 14 which is titled "Moving Beyond Spiritual Naiveté: Things You Wanted to Know About Satan, But Were Afraid to Ask."

Now, I'm not the kind of guy who sees the devil under every rock. But at times I've had to admit that I have observed a direct attack by Satan.

During the last ski season, the twelve-year-old son of one of our church members nearly died from a skiing accident. When his skis hit soft snow, he was catapulted through the air and struck a building, suffering severe head injuries.

As I stood in the hospital, praying with his folks, I knew in my heart that although Satan had not actually caused this accident, he did try to snatch that boy's life. Not only was he trying to snatch the boy's life away, but he was also trying to assault and discourage the boy's parents as much as possible, who are two very strong and wonderful believers in Christ.

I was delighted to grab that little guy's hand and pray, "Lord Jesus, we ask You to rebuke Satan and make sure he doesn't snatch this little life or receive any glory!" It felt very sound and good.

Now, not in every instance have I found myself praying in such a way. But I felt in that instance the enemy would take advantage of our suffering and turn the tables on us if he could.

I didn't want fear, indifference, denial or ignorance to give the enemy an advantage so I began to study the Bible and any commentaries I could get my hands on regarding enemy opposition. It was time to move beyond naiveté regarding spiritual matters.

The Bible made it very clear that Satan is real and that his desire is to destroy all that God loves. Satan is the origin of evil in the world and he is the source of most pain and suffering. The enemy would take advantage of us if he could. I certainly did not want our family to be devoured by the enemy's assault. Using the power and authority of the Lord Jesus Christ and with the leading of the Holy Spirit we needed to confront Satan head-on.

Who is authorized to perform spiritual warfare? I wondered. Spiritual warfare is available to all Christians. It's not a special gift given to a few. Matthew 16:18 says, "*The gates of Hell will not prevail against us.*"

Gary and I needed to recognize the strategies of the enemy, plan for warfare, then resist the enemy and refuse to cooperate with him. The Bible tells us that Satan's strategy is always the same—to steal, kill and destroy. Examining conditions, I believed the enemy's strategy against our family was recurring medical problems. If he could rob us of health and steal our joy he might create doubt or destroy our faith. The devil attacks weaknesses and attaches himself to those weaknesses. I John 5:19 says, "*The whole world is under the control of the evil one.*"

When I discovered the enemy's strategy I asked God to show us a plan. First I was led to I John 4:4, "*He that is in you is greater than he that is in the world.*" Then I studied the full armor of God in Ephesians 6:10-17. We needed to use the armor of God against the evil one, including the belt of truth, the breastplate of righteousness, the shoes fitted with readiness, the shield of faith, the helmet of salvation and the sword of the Spirit. We were to fight the enemy with the sword—God's Word that He has given us to bind the enemy. Our warfare needed to involve praying, worshipping, speaking and living in the Spirit.

We learned that we were given authority over Satan because Jesus is the King over all. Authority can be employed anytime we speak in the name of the Lord Jesus Christ. God extended His gifts to us. He empowered us with great authority through prayer and intercession.

One Scripture He gave us for encouragement is Deuteronomy 33:27, which says, *The eternal God is your refuge and underneath are the everlasting arms. He will drive out your enemy before you, saying, 'Destroy him!'*

Our new knowledge and commitment to God did not mean that life would be smooth sailing from then on. There would always be more to learn.

We had lived from crisis to crisis for several years. Subconsciously, crisis began to feel normal. This way of thinking contributed to our sons choosing a self-destructive path.

CHAPTER SIX

OUT OF DARKNESS

. . .you will weep and mourn, while the world rejoices.
You will grieve, but your grief will turn to joy.

JOHN 16:20

Families go through crisis in different ways. Some will be strengthened by crises; others will be destroyed. The difference is whom they trust in the midst of the storm.

The skiing injury caused extreme physical pain for Justin. He didn't remember anything about the accident, and his focus was on physical healing. Yet the rest of our family was experiencing deep emotional pain because we could see the difference in Justin. We had a more accurate insight into Justin's deficits. It was as if this accident happened to Gary, Nathan and me as well. Our dreams for the future were rearranged.

Grief wasn't something we anticipated. After all, there wasn't a funeral. Our son lived. But, we had no idea how to cope with the grief of losing the son we once had such high hopes for. Dealing with someone who sustained a head injury was something we knew almost nothing about

The social worker at the hospital encouraged us to attend meetings conducted by the Washington State Head Injury Foundation. We learned that there are not just head-injured individuals but rather head-injured families because the whole family is affected. You can't really tell someone is head-injured by looking at them. The brain-injured person wants to appear normal so they won't talk about it. Due to modern technology, people are surviving injuries they would have died from years ago. Society is not prepared and needs to be educated about this new minority group.

The group counseling sessions were extremely helpful. A family's emotional cycles were identified, and I saw how we fit into the stages. First, there was shock, panic and denial. I begged God to let Justin live from the moment I heard of the accident. Second, there was relief that he lived. As Justin emerged from the coma there was a false sense of hope. To show how little I knew about head injury, my biggest concern was that they had shaved his head, and we'd have to buy him a hat to wear to school. We grasped for hope that he would make progress, even though it was slow. Third, anger and depression became real with the understanding that he wasn't ever going to be the same. Mourning began. In our case, we grieved the loss of the son we once thought would become governor or win an Olympic gold medal. Finally, acceptance came with the recognition that our lives would never be the same. We began a new journey, learning about how to handle the effects of a serious head injury.

After years of constant crisis the foundations within our family began to crumble. Justin's injury was the worst of these crises. Emotionally, it seemed as if a cannon ball was blown through the strongest part of the wall. Through counseling we became aware that each of us had taken on displaced guilt.

A definition of guilt is the regret we experience when we choose to act in conflict with our conscience and beliefs. It is felt when we have control of a situation and don't follow through as we know we should, causing pain or inconvenience to someone else.

Displaced guilt can be irrational. When things happen that we have no control over—such as when someone is seriously injured or dies—feelings are displaced or transferred from the real source to another destructive behavior like drinking alcohol, smoking or taking drugs.

Each of us grieved differently.

After working for the church for three years Gary returned to working for the bank with a devotion to achieving the highest standards of excellence possible. The bank was one place that was safe, stable and dependable. His heart was not so exposed there. At work he was in control.

Gary felt responsible for my broken leg, even though it had been my decision to go night skiing on January 11, 1989.

"I shouldn't have let you go up there," he said. "I knew it was icy and unsafe."

Justin's accident was even more devastating to my husband. "Isn't it the father's responsibility to protect his family?" he said. This accident was beyond Gary's control, but it didn't stop him from feeling guilty about it. "I feel so helpless that I could not protect our son," he told me.

I became depressed and overly protective of both Justin and Nathan. If I was in control I thought I could keep my family safe. It was hard to maintain normalcy in our home. Displaced guilt was affecting me as pain burned deep in my heart. Hadn't I been the one who questioned God's willingness to answer prayers? Before the accident wasn't it I who confessed to my friend that I didn't know if my faith could withstand the loss of a family member? I felt responsible for Justin's accident. Maybe God made this accident happen to prove something to me.

So many questions still existed. Why would God allow my son to live but another child with a disease or injury to die?

Does God allow these things to happen? I wondered. After reading the book of Job, it certainly seemed He allowed Satan to kill Job's livestock, cause their home to collapse killing their children, and afflict Job with sores all over his body. Job couldn't see and hear what was taking place in the heavenly realm. Neither could I.

Even though Justin knew he would be on medication for the rest of his life, he lived in denial for many years, wanting to believe he was just like everyone else. It wasn't until years after his accident, when college and seeking a career became a challenge, that a frustrated Justin finally recognized his deficits and grieved his losses. When he was 22 he broke down and cried for three days.

Nathan suffered the most, I think. We didn't understand it at the time but he didn't know how to cope nor did he know how to express his needs.

CHAPTER SEVEN

WHY NOT ME?

Let us draw near to God with a sincere heart in full assurance of faith,
having our hearts sprinkled to cleanse us from a guilty conscience
and having our bodies washed with pure water.

HEBREWS 10:22

Nathan sat slouched on the couch, his hands and teeth clenched. It had been six years since his brother had been critically injured. He was now fourteen, but still struggled with his feelings about Justin's accident.

"Justin and I were supposed to be Olympic downhill racers," he told me with a wistful voice. The famous twin brothers Phil and Steve Mahre, who had both recently won Olympic medals in downhill racing, were from Washington and were my sons' heroes. "We were supposed to be the famous Scott brothers."

Justin was four years and one day older than Nathan, but after the accident it was as if their roles were reversed. Nathan became the older brother, helping Justin relearn how to feed himself, walk, read and practice appropriate social skills. Not many kids had experienced the crises Nathan had, and the stress of it made him old beyond his years.

Nathan was preoccupied internally with processing the turmoil around him and his performance at school suffered. Within just a few months of the accident, Nathan's teacher expressed her concern that he was falling behind in reading and spelling. There just didn't seem to be enough hours in the day nor the emotional energy for me to help him with homework. As hard as I tried to be sure Nathan was getting lots of attention with music lessons and sports; the focus remained on Justin. No one was at fault.

On March 25, 1989, the front page of the *Journal American* featured a photo and story about Justin. The media had given the accident a lot of coverage, in part because Justin had been participating in a ski school race at the time. Due to negligence on how the racecourse was set up, we were involved in a lawsuit against them. It was time consuming and stressful, and it put our family in the media spotlight.

We attended counseling as a family and stumbled through the next few years of emotional adjustments and litigation.

A gnawing sense of guilt growing within Nathan was mixed with jealousy. "Justin gets so much attention, I wish the accident had happened to me."

I thought I could reason with him.

"I can understand the jealousy, Nathan," I said as I put my hand on his shoulder. "Justin won the lawsuit and it may seem like a sizable amount. But, no amount of money could ever pay for what happened to him. Would you want to be brain injured and on medication the rest of your life?"

"No. Of course not, but why do so many bad things happen to our family when we are Christians?" Nathan asked.

All I could tell him was, "The Bible says, '*The rain falls on the just and the unjust.*' Being a Christian does not protect us from bad things happening, Nathan. If becoming a Christian put a protective bubble around us, everyone would become a believer. People would seek God not out of love and devotion, but out of safety. God does not want us to say we are believers because of what we will receive. He wants those who have a relationship with Him to stand on their faith, whether circumstances are good or bad."

I told Nathan the story in John 9:1-6 of the man who was born blind. The disciples asked Jesus, "Who sinned? The man or his parents?"

"Jesus told his disciples that neither the man nor his parents sinned, but the miracle they witnessed, as Jesus healed the blind man, was to glorify God."

Nathan frowned and went to his room.

Gary and I still didn't know how deeply troubled Nathan was.

It wasn't until ten years after the accident (when he was eighteen) that Gary and I learned through Nathan's counselor, that subconsciously, Nathan felt guilty because the accident hadn't happened to him. Nathan was present and gave his consent for the counselor to discuss this with us. He said, "An individual dealing with survivor guilt may have felt powerless at the time of the accident. Justin's skull had been shattered, but Nathan's spirit was crushed. Nathan's sense of safety and stability were devastated. In Nathan's case he attempts to punish himself in a variety of ways."

When I read about survivor guilt, returning to a familiar routine was recommended. Our family hadn't known what a regular routine was for several years. Crises occurred so often that visits to the hospital Emergency Room were routine. We were on a first-name basis with the hospital staff.

Nathan had trouble sleeping and often complained of nightmares. Memories haunted him. His frustration came out when he got into fights at school. Smoking cigarettes, marijuana, and abuse of alcohol helped dull the pain. Skipping school became a common occurrence.

Nathan was on a downward spiral until we transferred him to a small private Christian high school geared for kids at risk. With a teacher/pupil ratio of one to one they pushed, tutored and encouraged Nathan through his senior year. He also continued to see that wonderful, wise Christian counselor for another year. I thank God for placing counselors and teachers in Nathan's life who cared enough about him to not give up.

"We have been given a gift, Nathan," I reminded him. "Justin survived. Grieve for those who lose their brother, sister, mother or father. We did the best we could at the time. Thank you for your help during those times of disaster. Nathan, you were tremendously courageous for an eight-year-old."

"Thanks, Mom, but I didn't feel courageous at the time. I was just surviving from day to day."

CHAPTER EIGHT

TRAINING UP A CHILD

Train up a child in the way he should go,

and when he is old he will not depart from it.

PROVERBS 22:6

I had a problem with that verse. I always thought it said, "Train up a child in the way he should go, and he will not depart from it." One major problem was that I omitted the middle phrase, which says, "when he is old." That must mean there is a time in the middle when the child might "depart." When we had teenagers I began to cling to the promise of that verse, "and when he is old he will not depart from it." Hopefully it wouldn't be when they were too old.

Our boys were brought up going to church every Sunday. We had family Bible studies with our children, prayed before every meal and at bedtime. Justin and Nathan both attended Christian elementary schools.

Our sons could not have chosen a worse time to "depart" from the way He would have them go.

In January of 1995 my mother, who was 73 years old and my best friend, was dying of cancer. I drove five hours every Friday from Seattle, Washington, to Corvallis, Oregon, to spend the weekend and help with her care. During the week she received help from a friend as well as Hospice caregivers who came daily. My sister, Kathy and I often made the trip together. Kathy usually cleaned the cozy house or mowed the lawn while I cooked meals to put in the freezer. We helped bathe her, do laundry and monitor her medication chart.

Many hours were spent just sitting with Mom and talking when she was able. I listened with new interest to Mom's childhood stories of the depression years and growing up in the years before television.

My kind, gentle father had died unexpectedly three years earlier. Because of the suddenness and shock of his passing. I wanted to cherish every last memory with my mom. Every moment with her was precious.

But, my devotion to Mom began causing an emotional division. My husband and two sons also needed me at home. My boss at the physical therapy center where I worked was also concerned about the amount of time I was taking off work. My employer was understanding about my absence, but he also needed me in the office. My emotional resources were being stretched to the brink.

One Sunday night, I returned to Seattle utterly exhausted and wondered how much longer I could keep up these long weekend trips.

Gary greeted me solemnly, "We have to hold a family meeting." His voice and the look on the boys' faces told me this was not going to be a happy meeting.

"Over the weekend a friend told me that our sons are 'doing drugs,'" said Gary as he slumped into a chair in the living room. Justin was 18 and a senior in high school. Nathan was 14 and a freshman. The boys hesitatingly confessed that they were smoking pot. They did almost everything together, and we thought that brotherly bond was wonderful until we ran into this obstacle.

As I weighed this news my body started shaking uncontrollably. *I wonder if this is what it is like to have a nervous breakdown. How much can a person stand before they snap?* I wrapped myself in a blanket, tucked my feet under myself and curled up in one of my grandmother's old, blue, overstuffed chairs. My emotions swung from hurt, when tears turned to groaning that came from deep within my soul, to anger, when I would stand up and start shouting.

"How could you do this to us?" I cried. "*Why* would you do this?"

"Everybody does it." Nathan said defiantly. 'We didn't mean anything against you guys."

Justin said his older friends helped supply Nathan and his younger friends with marijuana. We later found out they experimented with a few other things, but "pot" and alcohol were their drugs of choice.

Would they be defiant and decide to move out? I feared.

As a mom, I couldn't stand the thought of my sons choosing not to respect our rules, and possibly choosing to live somewhere else. Why wouldn't Justin and Nathan choose the Christian morals and standards by which they had been raised?

"As a dad," Gary said, "I feel like a failure. I tried to be the perfect father. I attended every race, game and concert. I was on ski patrol so the family could ski at a reduced rate and stay up in the ski patrol lodge every weekend." At times Gary would sit in my dad's old recliner with his head in his hands. Suddenly, he would jump up and pace the length of the living room.

"Don't you understand?" Nathan said loudly. "It's not about you."

No. We didn't understand.

I used to say, "It's Saturday night and we know where our teenagers are. They're here with us or out skiing with friends."

Little did we know that was where they were "getting stoned" the most.

A friend tried to warn me once, but I was naïve. I didn't want to see. "My kids would never do drugs," I said, confidently.

Use of marijuana was largely why neither of them was doing well in school. Justin told us, "It's easy to get drugs anywhere, any time. It's not expensive. Friends often just give it to us."

Gary and I were stunned. Should we check both boys into an inpatient drug treatment program or kick them out? The next morning we sought family counsel. The counselor asked Justin and Nathan, "Do you want to remain living at home?"

"Yes," they said in unison as they stared at the floor in embarrassment.

"Are you willing to abide by the rules?"

"Uh, huh," they both mumbled quietly.

He advised us to enforce a program with AA (Alcohol Anonymous) or NA (Narcotics Anonymous) in which they would attend 90 meetings in 90 days.

Since I was extremely involved in caring for my dying mother, the responsibility of monitoring the boys and their recovery program fell heavily upon Gary. He bought them the AA books and policed their attendance. Time was spent with them talking and crying. When they began attending AA meetings they actually recognized some kids from school there as well. After 90 days we were convinced they were "cured."

"I love you both, and I want to live at home," Justin said.

"I'm so sorry, please forgive me," pleaded Nathan with big tears dropping onto his chest.

They completed the AA meetings and "went straight." Nathan continued to attend the meetings and wanted to hang around at school with the kids that were committed to their recovery. A counselor at school conducted an AA lunch group in which Nathan attended a few times a week.

By February of 1996 my sister and I physically could not continue the weekend trips to Oregon. Mom's health was quickly declining. As a result, we had to stay with her for longer periods of time. Even with the help of the Hospice program, Mom was not receiving the care she needed. She was moved to a hospital in Seattle for the final three weeks of her life, where she died peacefully.

After Mom's death I didn't have time to grieve. I had to go back to work. My employer needed me in the office and my income was certainly helpful. I was numb, but continued to function as if in a fog. Our sons' recovery programs were important, and I tried to get involved. We learned from the counselor that because our family had stumbled from crisis to crisis, we had never fully recovered from one trauma before the next one was upon us. Crisis began to feel normal in our household. Nathan's acute appendectomy, my fractured femur, Justin's head injury, Gary's kidney stones, losing both of my parents within three years of each other, three more revisions to my hip caused a very big pile of rubble that we didn't see accumulating. Each person's pain was deep, but we tried to go through the motions of a "normal " family." Alcohol and pot had been easy ways for our sons to dull their emotional pain.

Nathan spoke in front of his high school class about his decision to continue going to AA and to stay away from alcohol and drugs. They had lots of friends, and neither one of them ever lacked for a date.

It wasn't all bad. There were a lot of good times over the next few years. Our family still enjoyed weekends in the mountains together in the winter and had wonderful family vacations in the summer. We were close in many ways and did a lot of talking. The boys were always open about their latest girlfriend. Nathan always had a mischievous twinkle in his eye and made us laugh. He wasn't a great student, but got through on his charm. Next to the below average grade, his report cards always read, "Nathan is a delight to have in class."

The reprieve was short lived. I found out that Justin got "stoned" after his high school graduation and I told his dad. I said, "Let's forgive this one offense and excuse it as a 'graduation celebration.'" Gary agreed. Slowly I began to find out about parties, which I didn't tell Gary about. Justin was then caught on the University of Washington campus fleeing from a party and charged with "a minor in possession of alcohol." Gary did find out about that and was furious, but again I pleaded, "Hopefully he has learned his lesson."

But, about a month later, Justin and a friend were arrested in a park with marijuana. Legally, Justin was now an adult. "Let me handle it, Mom," he said defiantly. I didn't tell Gary and Justin "handled it."

Before long, I found out that Nathan, too, was partying and smoking marijuana again. I had them take Urinary Analysis (UA) tests, which proved that both boys were not using any other drug than marijuana and confirmed the count was low. Still, we had set a rule that we would not support any substance abuse.

Our town has a counseling center for teenagers so Nathan started going to a counselor on his own. He said he had a lot to work out. But, I also knew he continued to break the laws regarding drug and alcohol use. Both boys knew the family rules. Since Nathan was over 16, and Justin was now 20, I had no doubt that Gary *would* kick them both out if he found out.

I was being torn in half. I couldn't stand the thought of making our sons leave home. But by not telling Gary what his sons were doing I was deceiving my husband. I rationalized that I was protecting the family. *Gary had a stressful job at the bank and didn't need more pressure,* I reasoned.

This crisis affected my whole identity. I had devoted myself to being the perfect Christian mom. I scheduled my work to allow me to be home in the afternoons when the boys returned from school. I cooked them great meals, and I prided myself in keeping everyone's clothes clean and neat. People called us the Cleaver family from the TV show "Leave it to Beaver." But Justin and Nathan's bad choices caused me to make compromises that allowed Satan in the back door. I have found that sin begins with a compromise. Compromise is dangerous because it takes our minds off God and away from the Holy Spirit. Sin, by means of compromise, was so subtle we didn't realize it was happening.

Clinging to the promise in Proverbs 22:6 I reasoned that surely

Justin and Nathan would return to "the way they were trained." In fact, they were usually in church with us on Sundays. Justin still enjoyed studying his Bible. I believed God would bring them back. The boys just weren't ready to be out on their own—actually, I wasn't ready to "let go and let God."

When I turned to Colossians 2:5 and I Corinthians 14:40, I read that God is a God of order. The Word instructs us to submit to structure and authority. Even though they loved us, Justin and Nathan certainly were not willing to submit to rules and authority. Anything done outside of truth and righteousness can become an entry point for Satan. The devil only stops when Christians take authority over him in the name of the Lord Jesus Christ. We needed to learn the strategy of the enemy and stand aggressively against him.

I was trying to be an amateur substitute for God. John 3:30 says, *"He must increase but I must decrease."* Instead of decreasing, I was clutching harder to protect my sons. Later I learned that we should not interfere with what God is doing. In Matthew 10:34 I discovered that sometimes a life must be wrecked before it can be saved. It may crumble before it can be rebuilt.

Keeping the truth from Gary weighed on me and added to physical issues already attacking my body. The pain caused by arthritis in my hips and cervical spine grew worse each day. I was getting more and more depressed and losing the will to live. I still had not allowed myself to fully grieve the loss of my parents. Deceiving Gary was now killing me. He had been my best friend, my husband, my lover, my spiritual soul mate, and the father of our sons. Yet, I wasn't being honest with him. If only I had known my sin could have cost me everything.

I asked to meet Nathan's counselor, then arranged for our family to meet together with him the following week.

Before the counseling session I prayed, "Lord, the burden is getting too hard to bear. If our family falls apart I will blame myself. How can I live with that?" I asked with my stomach in knots.

During the family counseling session I told everything. Justin's party drinking and his arrest were exposed. Nathan's occasional return to marijuana (UA tests proved they were occasional) was uncovered. I asked Gary's forgiveness for withholding this information from him.

Nathan's counselor was a wonderful, wise, Christian man. As we sat in the comfortable office he tried to keep us calm. He tried to keep us from over-reacting. But it all blew up. Nathan stormed out in the middle of the session. He felt that I showed favoritism because I had "covered" for Justin and wouldn't cover for him. Gary was livid. I was crying.

Justin and Nathan had lied and had been deceptive as they broke house rules. I withheld information from Gary and covered for the boys. Gary was hurt and angry. We were all in sin. Ongoing sin opened the gate for the enemy.

When we got home there was a lot of shouting. Gary felt betrayed by the whole family. The kids had broken the rules, and I had covered for them.

Gary was so distraught he said and did many hurtful things. Pictures were torn up and physical things were wrecked. Hearts were broken.

"I have spent 27 years supporting this family and I'm tired… done… finished. I'm going away, and I never want to see any of you again."

The kids were given a deadline to be out in two weeks and Gary wanted a divorce. We would sell the house, and then go our separate ways. Gary was reacting out of pain, anger and his feelings of failure. No one could escape.

The fallout from the blast devastated me.

One day after this incident, I was so overwhelmed I went out in the yard and lay in the grass and wept bitter tears for a long time. Finally, I cried out to my Heavenly Father. "Oh, God," I sobbed. "Once again I turn to you for strength. I can't imagine life without Gary and the boys. Please help us. It's going to take a miracle to rebuild our family. It seems beyond hope. Only you can perform what looks to me like the impossible."

The next two weeks the boys spent all their spare time looking in the newspapers for places to live. Our house was very quiet as we each tried to avoid looking at each other, hoping there wouldn't be another explosion. Gary and I had an appointment with a realtor so we could put the house up for sale. Emotionally, I was so tired I felt like I was just functioning on autopilot. We were beginning to sort our material possessions out and box thing up.

I found myself praying constantly: "God you have given me strength in every crisis we have been through."

Every day I gained confidence that if the rest of the family separated my faith in God would remain strong. None of this was God's fault. We made bad choices, now we had to live with the consequences. I told myself that if Gary left I would understand, and I would always love him. The boys and I would stay in touch.

CHAPTER NINE

ONE DAY FROM DESTRUCTION

But the one who hears my words and does not put them into practice
is like a man who built a house on the ground without a foundation.
The moment the torrent struck that house,
it collapsed and its destruction was complete.

LUKE 6:49

On July 22, 1998, we were one day from splitting up. We had been battered by 10 years of torrential rains that finally caused our spiritual foundation to collapse. The deadline was set for the boys to move out by the end of the next day. Gary and I were going to separate as soon as the house sold.

Our family was crumbling into a heap of rubble. In Jeremiah 4:10 it says that there was so much rubble the Jews couldn't even see how to begin the process of rebuilding Jerusalem and the wall surrounding it.

The rebuilding of our family seemed impossible also. We had crumbled into such a heap of rubble I couldn't see how to begin the rebuilding process. *We've experienced miracles before, but it's is going to take a really big one this time,* I thought.

God was in control and had to get our attention. We thought things couldn't get any worse...they did!

Nathan came home at 2 p.m. when he was supposed to be at the YMCA teaching swimming lessons. He was gray and shaking. As soon as I saw him I knew something terrible had happened. He collapsed on the living room floor sobbing. Through his anguished cries he told me that he had been falsely accused of touching a little girl inappropriately during a swimming lesson and had been put on leave from work pending investigation.

I called Gary at work and told him there was an emergency, and he needed to come home immediately.

"I've got work to do," snapped Gary. "I'm sick of our family always having some crisis, and I'm expected to drop everything to run home."

I could hardly talk, but through sobs and gulps of air I begged, "Gary please... You must come home. This is really bad."

When Gary got home he slammed the front door and threw his briefcase in the old recliner. "OK, I'm here. What is it this time?" he said sternly, standing straight and tall—arms folded across his chest.

The story began to unfold. Nathan had arrived at work and the Director of the Y called him into her office. The Aquatics Director was already there as well.

Nathan said, "I was so excited because I just knew they were both there to tell me I would be getting a promotion or a raise."

"Good afternoon, ladies," he greeted them happily, but got solemn responses.

The Director informed Nathan that he had been accused of touching a little girl in a personal place during a swimming lesson. He said his legs couldn't support him, and he crumbled to his knees right in her office. Nathan's boss phoned the police and the CPA (Child Protective

Agency). Pending further investigation Nathan was suspended from his job, and he wouldn't be allowed to apply for any other job. The case was to be dismissed or Nathan would be charged with a crime.

Before he left, Nathan turned back and told them he did not do this hideous thing.

As Gary was given this awful news, his spirit melted within him. No longer was he upset that he had fathered a dysfunctional family—one that was on the very edge of breaking up. His heart was broken for his son. His only thought was that his innocent son was being accused of a crime he did not commit.

Through tears Nathan apologized to us. "I'm so sorry for doing drugs. I didn't mean to hurt you."

"Please believe that I would never commit such a disgusting act as the one I've been accused of," he reassured us again.

In that moment all former sins were forgiven and forgotten. The slate was wiped clean. Once again Gary became the spiritual head of our household, and the battle began against an enemy who hates to see families restored.

Gary threw his arms around Nathan—then we all embraced, sobbing. Our children didn't always do things our way, but we knew Nathan would never harm a child. We believed him.

Gary broke down and cried with his head in his hands. As he sat next to Nathan on the couch he said, "I'm so sorry for all the angry things I've done these last two weeks and all the terrible things I've said. Please forgive me."

Nathan was crying so hard he couldn't talk, but he nodded his head.

"I will mortgage the house and sell everything we have to defend you, son. Nothing we own is as important as your freedom and our relationship as a family. We need to put on the armor of God and stand aggressively against the enemy," Gary said. "Father God once saw his children in sin and sent His son to be an example to the world. His son was falsely accused and judged. His son was tried to set the world free of their sins forever. God will stand beside our family."

When Justin came home from work we told him about the accusation against Nathan. We all cried and hugged each other again in a way that had been a part of our family since the boys were little—"the family hug." We talked more and Gary led us in a prayer together. "Thank you, Heavenly Father, for opening our eyes and showing us that our family is valuable in your sight. We praise you for your abounding mercy."

"If this is what it took to put our family back together, then I'm willing to go through this, even if I have to go to prison like Joseph in the Bible," Nathan said as he once again clung hard to our necks. Tears ran down his face as he prayed, "Thank you God for this miracle. If I have to go to jail I'll praise you for parents who can keep forgiving."

Like Joseph, Nathan was never angry or bitter against those who falsely accused him. Instead, he declared it a miracle from God to put our family back together. In Genesis 39, Potiphar's wife tried to seduce Joseph, and when he refused, Potiphar's wife made false accusations about him. Joseph was thrown in prison. He could have been bitter, but he saw that God could turn his painful situation for good.

We too were hurting, but we finally realized how much we loved each other and how important it was to fight to save our family. We would sacrifice everything to help one of our own. Thus the wounds of our hurting family began to heal and I started to see a flicker of hope.

As Joseph said to his brothers in Genesis 50:20, *"You intended to harm me [by selling him into slavery], but God intended it for good."* Satan may have intended to break up our family, but God had the power to change these events to good. That day our family was restored.

During the next year Nathan would have to walk through the fire, but he did not walk through it alone. We would walk through it as a family.

Gary then shared an experience he had earlier in the month. While doing his daily Bible study he was led to Psalm 35. He didn't know then, but now understood why it had been on his heart, and we read it daily as a family over the next several months.

Contend, O LORD, with those who contend with me;
fight against those who fight against me.
Take up shield and buckler;
arise and come to my aid.

Brandish spear and javelin
against those who pursue me.
Say to my soul,
"I am your salvation."

May those who seek my life
be disgraced and put to shame;
may those who plot my ruin
be turned back in dismay.

May they be like chaff before the wind,
with the angel of the LORD driving them away...

Ruthless witnesses come forward;
they question me on things I know nothing about.

They repay me evil for good
and leave my soul forlorn...

O LORD, you have seen this; be not silent.
Do not be far from me, O Lord.

Awake, and rise to my defense!
Contend for me, my God and Lord.

NIV

The Living Bible reads:

"Rise up, O Lord my God; vindicate me. Declare me 'not guilty,' for you are just."

This became our family prayer for Nathan. Surely God would vindicate him for He is a just God. We had to keep our eyes on the cross and remember that in all things, circumstances and situations, His purposes will be served and fulfilled, even when the "training up of a child" seems unbearable. The miracle of trials is His grace to join us right where we are.

CHAPTER TEN

REFINER'S FIRE

Though now for a little while you may have had to suffer grief in
all kinds of trials. These have come so that your faith—of greater
worth than gold, which perishes even though refined by fire—
may be proven genuine and may result in praise,
glory and honor when Jesus Christ is revealed.

I PETER 1:7

In January of 1998 Nathan graduated early from a small Christian high school with a Rotary Club scholarship to our local community college. In June when he walked down the aisle for graduation with the rest of his high school classmates, Nathan had already completed one quarter of college. Majoring in Recreational Education, he made the Dean's Honor List his first two quarters of college. Quite a change from high school.

We were unable to find out the details of the allegations made against him for months. The accused have no rights. Nathan was not allowed to know who accused him, what he was accused of, or any circumstances regarding the incident. The law is written to protect the accuser, especially if it's a child. There were no witnesses, nor was there any evidence. It was a case of one person's word against the other…one was a child and the other an adult.

A detective from the local police department informed us that they would interview the girl and her mother, then the case would be dismissed or Nathan would be charged. The Director of the YMCA informed us that these things usually only take a few days. While our lives hung in suspense, the detective took 10 days before he interviewed the girl who claimed Nathan touched her inappropriately during a swim lesson.

Nathan's counselor advised us to hire a defense attorney immediately. Nathan needed his family and good legal advice. Possibly an attorney could speed up the process. I researched lawyers in Seattle and hired the best defense attorney I could find. He contacted the Police Department and was able to find out a few more details.

In a slow and agonizing way the days turned into weeks. Each time I called, Nathan's boss informed me that it was still under investigation. Yet, there was no charge, nor was there a dismissal. Nathan remained on unpaid suspended leave.

The detective couldn't file a charge until he had interviewed Nathan and given him a chance to tell his side. Our attorney repeatedly asked for this interview…days dragged on. Finally, a month after the alleged incident the detective set up an interview with Nathan, and his attorney.

Nathan was then told that the supposed offence occurred on July 21, 1998 and he was shown a picture of the girl making the accusation. Five times a day Nathan taught swimming lessons to six or eight wet, wiggling children. (I will use the name Lisa Smith for his accuser in the rest of the story, because she is still a minor.) He did not recognize the girl from her school picture.

Many people were present when the alleged crime occurred. The

YMCA swimming pool is like a fish bowl. A huge glass window overlooks the pool. Anyone coming into the Y can see everyone in the pool and there are always people standing at the picture window...yet no one heard or saw anything suspicious. We thought after the interview with the detective the case surely would be dropped. It was not.

Nathan continued his college courses in the fall and continued to get good grades, but stress was beginning to wear on him. He was not eating well, and he was unable to sleep.

Our attorney encouraged Nathan to undergo a polygraph test. Possibly this would convince the Prosecuting Attorney's office of his innocence and sway them to dismiss the case. Although it would be very expensive and emotionally taxing, we agreed that if it would help Nathan's case it would be worth the price.

When Nathan got home from the polygraph test he looked sick as nausea and dizziness swept over him. He was gray, sweating and shaking. "I feel like I'm going to throw up," Nathan said as he entered our front door. "I don't think I passed the test," he said. "My heart was racing and I was so nervous I thought I might pass out."

Nathan described the polygraph test. They asked him extremely personal questions. He said, "I was even asked sexual questions I didn't understand and had to ask them to explain." Looking thoroughly exhausted, Nathan went up to his room to rest.

Later, when I was alone, I cried for what my son had to go through. *Would the refiner's fire prove Nathan genuine and glorify God,* I wondered. *Did this young girl know the cost to our family emotionally, physically and financially?*

The next few hours were a blur of tears, panic and fear as time crawled by. We finally got a call from our attorney with the polygraph results...Nathan passed with flying colors! We rejoiced with Nathan. Surely now, the prosecutor would know that Nathan could not have committed this crime and the case would be dismissed.

Thanksgiving came and went and Nathan was not charged, nor

was he dismissed. Four months had passed since being suspended from his job and not allowed to apply for another job while a criminal case was pending.

Nathan finished the fall quarter and wondered whether to change his major. He was serving God through street ministry, working at the church with the Junior High group and majoring in Recreational Education because he saw a need to help kids. Once Nathan's passion, he now feared working with children.

Christmas came and went. Hopefully, the New Year would bring good news. Surely he could have a fresh start in 1999. We prayed that truth would prevail.

We watched Nathan as he anguished through this process. Jail or prison became very real and terrifying possibilities, but his faith grew as he learned to trust in God. From the very first day he said that if this event was what it took to reunite our family then it was all worth it. We clung to each other for support. Our family felt alone, however.

When one of us was hurt or ill in the past, our church, relatives and friends surrounded us. We always knew others were praying for us. This was different. Only a few close friends could be told. People sometimes make judgments without knowing all the facts. As we slowly told our closest relatives and friends, they wept with us. Those who knew Nathan well believed him and loved him.

Since he couldn't continue his job at the Y, Nathan took on yard jobs. This turned out to be a real blessing. Many people in our affluent community had beautifully landscaped yards, and Nathan learned a lot about gardening. Nathan said, "I don't think of myself as a scholar, I think of myself as a sponge." It was true. He soaked up what he heard on the TV's Discovery channel, what people taught him while gardening and landscaping and by watching those more experienced than he. Nathan found a new love…horticulture and landscape architecture.

Nathan continued college during the winter quarter but was becoming more and more depressed about the case hanging over his head. He couldn't concentrate on homework. It was a struggle just to get through each day. He still wasn't eating or sleeping well.

On March 11, 1999, ten years to the day from Justin's head injury accident, Nathan was charged with a gross misdemeanor. We couldn't believe it! Fully unprepared for the arraignment, we walked into a courtroom in which the judge, court reporter, attorneys and their clients went through a door to the front, while the rest of the courtroom was separated with a bulletproof glass wall. We sat on benches behind the glass wall and listened to the proceedings on a speaker.

Most cases had to do with drugs. Those being charged had to sit on a separate bench. Nathan was directed to join that group. He was asked to remove his wallet, things in his pockets, rings, jewelry or personal possessions and place them in a paper bag. He, along with the others, had to place his hands behind his back and was handcuffed. As we watched from behind a glass wall, our son was led away to the county jail. We couldn't hug or touch him. Nathan looked over at us as he was led away. I mouthed, "I love you," with tears streaming down my face. Those charged would be photographed, fingerprinted and then either held or released on bond.

We waited several hours for Nathan's release. Later, he told us about being led in front of all the other prisoners in their cells and the "trash talk" they shouted at these new inmates. He was put in a holding cell with eight other men. The cell was totally enclosed except for one small 3" by 5" window in the door. There was a commode and small sink in the corner, and one bench that two men could sit on. The others had to stand. Most of the other men had been through this before and discussed their previous experiences and prison terms. The air was foul and close.

At one point Nathan picked up what looked like a playing card with a string tied around it. A large black man told him, "Hey man, never pick up nothin' off the prison floor. Drop that in the toilet and wash your hands."

Innocently Nathan said, "It's just a playing card—a King of hearts—with a string tied around it."

The man replied, "It was probably a crack pipe."

Nathan smelled it and agreed.

"Now, drop it in the toilet, flush it and wash your hands," said the man, kindly. "You don't know where that's been. Don't never pick up nothin' off the prison floor, dude."

Nathan did as he was told and spent the rest of the afternoon standing in the corner listening to their tales.

Finally, after everyone had been processed Nathan was released until his trial, which was set for June. Nathan said he felt so filthy he just wanted to go home as fast as he could to shower and change clothes.

"If I ever know of any kid who even thinks of smoking pot or doing anything remotely illegal I will tell them about spending one day in jail," he said. "I certainly never want to step foot in that place again."

A restraining order forbade Nathan from being anywhere children might be unattended, including parks, malls and even the gym we had belonged to since Nathan was eight years old.

One evening I was left alone, and I found myself becoming so angry I wanted to punch someone or something. This all seemed so unjust! It stole away whatever youthful innocence Nathan still had. Only God could repair the scars being left on his spirit. I cried out to Him, "Please help us to know what to do. We are desperate for your wisdom. God, please protect and comfort our son."

Our attorney had not been allowed to interview Lisa Smith until Nathan was charged. Now our attorney and a private investigator were able to set up the interviews. They were to be held in the office of the Deputy Prosecuting Attorney. The first appointment was "for-gotten" by the girl and her mom. One of them was ill the following week. (Of course, each time one of these meetings was set up we were paying our attorney and private investigator for their time to go to the Prosecuting Attorney's office.) Finally, the interview was conducted.

The story changed from the time Lisa was first interviewed by the detective. It changed again during the interview by the Prosecuting Attorney. However, our attorney said the girl presented well, was mature and articulate, dressed well, and spoke clearly for an eight-year-old. There was no hesitancy on her part to discuss sex or anything about the case.

For the spring quarter Nathan took a break from college. His trial was scheduled for late May, or early June, and he would have to miss a week of school just before finals. Besides, trial preparation took quite a bit of time and energy.

As the trial drew closer, Nathan's stress level soared and he was getting very scared. At different times we were each falling apart. It was as if we were adrift in a stormy sea of emotions. We took turns holding each other up. Gary was having a difficult time concentrating on work. So I took him away for a weekend hoping a complete change of scenery would get rid of the stress. It worked…but only until we got back home. Then it was all still there waiting for us.

In the middle of May we decided Nathan needed to get away from everything. He wanted to go to Eugene, Oregon, where he was born, to fish in the McKenzie River. (We named him Nathan McKenzie after this mighty, rushing river.) Nathan especially wanted to visit our dear, long-time neighborhood friends.

Nathan stood on the bank and fished for hours, soaking in the serenity of that special place. We drove him past our old house and showed him around Eugene. He kept talking about how good it felt to be there.

Saturday night after dinner we were cleaning up dishes when Nathan said, "Do you realize one month from today I will be free or I will be in prison?"

We thought we had taken him away to a place where he could relax and forget the upcoming trial. There was no place on earth we could have taken him where he could have forgotten. He did, however, find refuge in the love of friends who believed in Nathan and shared our faith in a just and loving God.

On Sunday, Nathan wanted to worship at Faith Center, the church in which he was raised. I wasn't sure I could sit through a service at our old church without completely falling apart, but I said I would do it for him.

Even though Nathan was only four years old when we moved away from Eugene, he turned to me during the service and said, "How could you not feel like this is home?" In that service it seemed as if Jesus Himself had applied the balm of Gilead to Nathan's emotional wounds. He was ready to go back home and face the trial.

Before trial, Gary and I sought the counsel of our compassionate Pastor, Jerry Cook. He reminded us that Jesus repeatedly told his disciples, "Fear not."

Jerry said that all too often we allow our fears to become reality and we expend too much energy worrying about what "might happen." Self-talk could create a reality that did not exist. Jerry taught us to shorten decision-making time and deal only with the facts we knew to be true at that particular moment, hour or day. We were also warned about listening to "words from the Lord" or "advice" from well-meaning friends.

"If it's important and God wants you to hear something He'll tell you Himself. If the word is from the Lord, or the advice sound, check it against James 3:17-18,

> *The wisdom that comes from heaven is first of all pure; then peace-loving, considerate, submissive, full of mercy and good fruit, impartial and sincere. Peacemakers who sow in peace raise a harvest of righteousness.*

It was reassuring when Jerry said he would sit through the trial with us. He reminded us that we needed to rest in God's love. Our Father God wouldn't let us down. He is the God of miracles.

There is going to come a time of testing at Christ's Judgment Day to see what kind of material each builder has used. Everyone's work will be put through the fire so that all can see whether or not it keeps its value, and what was really accomplished.

I CORINTHIANS 3:13

CHAPTER ELEVEN

MOUNTAINS OF GRACE

From the fullness of His grace we have all received one
blessing after another. For the law was given through Moses,
grace and truth came through Jesus Christ.

JOHN 1:17-18

The Friday night before Nathan's trial was to begin, our church sponsored a free concert for the community, featuring recording artist Bob Fitts, Jr. from Kona, Hawaii. We had never heard of him, but decided to go just to get our minds off of the trial for a few hours.

I had been asking God for a sign that He heard us and was with us. *God I need a neon sign this time,* I prayed. I couldn't have imagined how much that encounter with Bob Fitts would change our lives.

Bob played and sang contemporary Christian praise music, which was soothing to my soul. Near the end of the concert, he made an altar call, asking those to come forward who were hurting and needed prayer. Many knelt on the steps and I was among them, tears streaming down my face. Bob sang a beautiful song about Jesus' love then prayed for us.

Gary put his arm around me as I leaned my head on his shoulder as I returned to my seat. Another song began and about two measures into it, he stopped. Bob told the audience he was sorry to stop the concert, but he had to talk to someone.

Looking directly at me, Bob asked, "What's your name?"

I was too embarrassed and astonished to reply. Gary shouted, "Barbara."

Bob said, "I sense God wants to tell you He will heap grace upon you. Not only a little grace, but mountains and mountains of grace will be heaped upon you and your family."

"I don't know what you are going through, but God wants you to understand, He knows your pain and His timing is perfect," he said soothingly.

I was crying so hard that I don't think I heard anything else he said. Nor did I hear the next song. *It was as if God talked directly to me through Bob Fitts, Jr.,* I thought. *This must be the neon sign I prayed for.* My heart knew it was the voice of God. In the true sense of the word it was awesome. God gave me comfort and assurance when I needed it the most, and I felt incredibly blessed. After that night I didn't doubt His presence and I knew, through God, all things are possible.

Bob said he wanted to meet with us after the concert where we received much encouragement and exchanged e-mail addresses. We stayed in touch for years to come and found out stopping the concert to give a prophecy is something he has rarely done.

Saturday morning I was still pondering what Bob had said. I didn't completely understand what it meant that God would heap mountains of grace upon our family. *What exactly is grace?* I wondered. *And what's the difference between mercy and grace?*

That evening at dinner I shared our experience at the concert with Justin and Nathan.

"I don't understand the difference between mercy and grace. Can you explain what that means?" I asked Gary.

"Yeah," Justin agreed. "I'm confused by that also."

"We need a family Bible study," Nathan agreed.

"Mercy is God not giving us what we deserve," Gary explained to three blank stares. Justin, Nathan and I still didn't get it. "Well, we all really deserve hell," Gary continued. "In Romans 3:23 it says, 'all have sinned and fall short of the glory of God.'"

"OK, I get that part," I said. "Now, what is grace?"

Gary was earnest. "Grace is God giving us what we don't deserve." But again, he received three confused looks. "We don't deserve heaven, but God loves us so much and wants an intimate relationship with us. Little kids think they should get rewards for good behavior. Well, we can't earn our way into heaven by good behavior."

Light was beginning to dawn on our faces.

Gary tried to help us understand. He read Ephesians 2:8, *"For it is by grace you have been saved, through faith—and this not from yourselves, it is the gift of God—not by works, so that no one can boast."*

"I get it now," I said. Justin and Nathan nodded in agreement. "God isn't basing His love for us on our good performance. He is reassuring us that He loves our family because of who He is, not because of who we are. It's hard to fathom a God who loves our family so much. We certainly don't deserve eternity with Him by the way we were treating each other about eleven months ago. I'm so grateful for such a loving God. Knowing about grace and mercy is liberating. I feel like no matter which direction Nathan's trial goes, God will heap grace upon our family. We will survive either way."

On Sunday our family all went to different places. We each needed time alone, just to think. It was the night before Nathan's trial, and Gary asked that our family gather together at 9:00 that evening for prayer. Justin, Nathan and I walked into the house together on that cold, rainy June evening. Gary had a fire going in the fireplace, and communion was set on the coffee table. There was a plate with a large, round loaf of bread and four glasses of grape juice waiting for us. In the center of the table Gary had three candles lit representing the Father, Son and Holy Spirit.

We prayed over Nathan and cried together. Gary then read the story of the Last Supper from Matthew and we took communion together.

I talked to the boys about being ready for battle and asked Gary to teach them about the whole armor of God from Ephesians 6:11-13. It wasn't the first time our sons heard this lesson, but Gary told them again about the belt of truth, the breastplate of righteousness, the shoes of readiness to spread the good news, the shield of faith, the helmet of salvation and the sword of the Spirit of God's word. These resources are available to all who follow Christ.

Gary adopted an encouraging tone. "All Christians have this equipment and should never take it off. Combat equipment of a Christian soldier is needed to fight spiritual warfare." We were ready for battle.

Monday morning was cool and sunny when we met our attorney. The three of us walked over to the towering courthouse in downtown Seattle. Homeless, street people laying and sitting on the steps outside were a sharp contrast to the well-dressed, briefcase-toting attorneys all headed for courtrooms and offices inside. Hard leather shoes echoed against the marble floor of the huge foyer.

The Deputy Prosecuting Attorney (DPA) had asked the Supervisor of the Assault team if this case should be dismissed due to the inconsistencies in Lisa Smith's statements, but he had not received an answer. First, Nathan was to be assigned a judge and then jury selection would begin. The trial could not begin until the DPA and his Supervisor made a decision regarding dismissal. Our attorney met with the two prosecuting attorneys in an office while we waited.

About thirty minutes later Nathan's attorney came out with a smile on his face and said, "I think we have good news, but Nathan, you have some decisions to make."

The PA's office offered a lesser charge of a misdemeanor in the 4th degree, but our attorney already told them Nathan would not settle for that because he did not commit any crime.

Next they offered something called an Alfred Plea, in which Nathan could agree to accept a misdemeanor to avoid trial, but for the record he would be allowed to say he was innocent. Nathan would be put on probation and have to do some community service work. Again, our attorney said his client would not agree to those charges.

Their final offer was to dismiss the case if Nathan would agree to take a sexual neuro-psychological evaluation within thirty days and they would be allowed thirteen years on the statute of limitations, when the girl would be twenty-one. His file would be kept open and if any criminal act took place during the next thirteen years, Nathan could be charged with a new crime along with this one being reopened.

We were sent to a small room in the courthouse library. Two hours were given to Nathan to make up his mind whether to accept these terms of dismissal or go to trial. He wanted to go to trial and prove his innocence before the girl, her family, his former employers and the Prosecuting Attorney. Nathan wanted to hear the judge's gavel and to hear the judge declare his innocence.

Our attorney explained the risks of going to trial. The PA's could increase the charges to two counts of misdemeanor. They could increase the charges to a felony in which the judge is obligated to sentence five to seven years in prison with this particular charge. A unanimous decision is necessary to win. If there was one person out of the twelve in the jury that did not agree, it would end in a "hung jury," and we would start all over.

They had taken nearly a year to get to this point and they gave Nathan only two hours! The decision had to be made by noon. Gary told them, "Nathan will be allowed every minute of the two hours. He will have an answer for you at 11:59 AM."

The stakes were high, but Nathan still wanted to go to trial. He said, "I hope they do charge me with a felony. Then they not only have to prove it happened, they have to prove I did it 'with intent.'" He was not willing to compromise.

Gary and I told Nathan that we loved him. His dad helped him write out all the plusses and minuses on paper for dismissal or for trial. We could not make that decision for him. It was a decision Nathan would have to live with the rest of his life. The decision needed to be his. We would back him up, and we would be there no matter what the outcome.

Nathan agonized for two hours. He was shaking so bad he said he felt sick to the stomach. Then he got the chills. I put my head down on the table and prayed for him. (We later learned that my sister was praying for him non-stop all morning and several other friends were fasting for him.) Our attorney came in and once again went over the risks.

All of a sudden, Nathan stood up and declared, "I'll accept their terms for dismissal."

Gary went around the table. Nathan embraced his dad and they cried together. I had tears streaming down my face while our attorney reached over and patted my shoulder.

"Is it over now?" Nathan asked.

"They will have to draw up the papers. Then tomorrow we will have to appear before a judge and all parties will sign the dismissal. It will be over by 9:30 tomorrow morning. You'll be free."

We still needed to learn more about God's mercy and grace.

CHAPTER TWELVE

FREED AND RELEASED

The Spirit of the Sovereign Lord is on me, because the Lord has anointed me to preach good news to the poor. He has sent me to bind up the brokenhearted, to proclaim freedom for the captives and release from darkness for the prisoners, to proclaim the year of the Lord's favor and the day of vengeance of our God, to comfort all who mourn, and provide for those who grieve in Zion—to bestow on them a crown of beauty instead of ashes, the oil of gladness instead of mourning, and a garment of praise instead of a spirit of despair. They will be called oaks of righteousness, a planting of the Lord for the display of his splendor.

ISAIAH 61:1-3

What were we supposed to do now? We had spent as much money on Nathan's defense as it cost to purchase our first house. The last year was consumed by his court case. I thought we'd come out of the courthouse dancing and rejoicing, but we didn't. Nathan had matured beyond his years in that long, drawn-out eleven months. Gary was quiet and looked sad. I was just plain exhausted.

When we stepped out of the dark courthouse onto the sunny streets of Seattle on June 6, 1999, I turned to our attorney and asked, "What now?"

"You resume your lives and go on."

"But can't we counter sue for slander or something, to cover our expenses?"

"When a child accuses an adult of molestation, the police have to be notified. In this case, normal procedures were followed. You have to let it go."

"Can't I at least write a letter?" I pleaded. "I don't think Lisa Smith, her family, or Nathan's employer have any idea what it cost us financially and emotionally."

Our attorney stopped to face me. "I have defended innocent men who were convicted of much more serious crimes and sent to prison. They lost their businesses, their homes and their families. After spending years in prison they walked out and asked me the same question. I had to tell them to start over and begin a new life.

"For Nathan it's over. There will be no jail. He's free from any more restrictions." He looked at Nathan kindly. "You are free to go anywhere. Return to college and leave this all behind."

When we reached the law office we shook hands and thanked our attorney. It was due to God, a good lawyer and a legal system, which finally worked that Nathan was free. We went home quietly.

What we didn't know was that God was going to heap more grace upon Nathan's decision and unwillingness to compromise.

Gary and Nathan joined the attorney the next morning for what was to be a five-minute court appearance. By this time I was so exhausted I chose to stay home. Our attorney was not pleased with the wording on the final dismissal papers. He said he would meet with the DPA (Deputy Prosecuting Attorney) and his supervisor and return in a few minutes. Fifteen minutes went by and the judge looked at Gary, who shrugged his shoulders. Thirty minutes…forty-five. After an hour the attorneys returned. Our attorney was smiling. He made them do a lot of reading in legal books but, they lowered the statute of limitation to two years and one year was already used up. They were also forced to allow our attorney to choose the psychologist who would perform the neuro-psychological test. The papers were signed. Alleluia! Case dismissed! His Truth did prevail!

Blessed is the man upon who perseveres under trial, because when he has stood the test he will receive the crown of life that God has promised to those who love Him.

JAMES 1:12

Nathan said, "The first thing I want to do is go to Chism Beach," a beautiful park on Lake Washington.

It had warmed up and was a beautiful day. Nathan went home and changed into shorts. Then he told me the afternoon was spent laying in the lush, green grass, staring up at azure skies and enjoying the fresh breezes off the lake.

"It feels so good to be free at last," he said when he returned home, with a big smile on his face, showing his straight white teeth. It had been so long since I had seen Nathan's warm smile that lights up his hazel eyes. It seemed as if weight was falling from his shoulders.

I called relatives and friends who supported us through this ordeal. They all cried tears of joy and relief with us. "When is the victory party?" many asked.

So the following Sunday afternoon we had an open house with a picnic in our front yard. I ordered a sheet cake decorated with a cross made of yellow roses trimmed in purple. The wording on the cake said, "Free at Last, Victory in Jesus." The weather was beautiful. It felt so good to sit in folding chairs on the lawn and give God the glory for His amazing mercy and grace.

Our friends wanted us to retell the whole story. Some had heard pieces, but they wanted to hear it all. We got in a circle and told of the ordeal from beginning to end.

"I wanted to be declared innocent in a court of law," Nathan told them. "But all of a sudden I realized these were courts of the world—courts of men. Men and their courts would vanish. I had already been found innocent before God. That is for eternity!"

Cheers of joy echoed through the tall Douglas fir trees surrounding our home.

Gary returned to his job at the bank. He had taken time off and had a lot of work to catch up on. Nathan resumed his college education, changing his major to horticulture. Justin had a job and got an apartment with a friend.

Would life return to normal? I wondered. *What's normal anyhow?*

I carried on with my schedule of gardening, housekeeping, playing my flute in a symphony, a chamber group, at church and teaching private lessons.

However, anger and bitterness were consuming me. Nagging thoughts always gnawed at the back of my mind. Every time I went to the grocery store or the mall I would look at young girls and wonder if one of them might be the one who caused us so much grief.

A friend of mine who owns her own family counseling practice gave me some insight: "You have no idea what kind of a life this girl has had. Maybe a painful childhood or a traumatic event caused a desire to hurt someone else."

We could only speculate as to what would motivate this girl to try to destroy another's life. "There's a saying that *hurting people, hurt people.* Something caused this girl to want to hurt another," said my friend. This discussion changed my preoccupation with, "Why would someone do this?" into a more constructive behavior... praying. I prayed Lisa's family would seek counseling. What Nathan's accusers really needed was a personal relationship with Jesus Christ, and now I prayed for the Smith family.

Bob Fitts, Jr., who had prophesied over me at his concert the Friday night before Nathan's trial, e-mailed us. He told us about a missionary organization called Youth With a Mission (YWAM). There were over 500 training bases around the world at that time, but the headquarters was in Kona, Hawaii, where he lived. He encouraged us to come to Hawaii, investigate YWAM, listen to some class lectures and attend church there."

"Your family needs rest. Come and sit at the feet of Jesus and be healed," he invited.

Over the next month and a half Gary and I discussed Bob's invitation. We realized how the accusations against Nathan and the events leading up to the possible trial had changed us.

Looking around our large, nicely furnished living room Gary said, "I've spent nearly 30 years working for a big house, cars, skis and 'stuff.' None of it is important any more...I would have cashed in all of our savings, mortgaged our home and sold everything for our son's freedom." I agreed. Through Nathan's trial we gained a whole new perspective on life. Priorities changed and relationships magnified.

Now we wanted to get rid of everything to allow us the freedom to follow God. He had blessed us so incredibly. Our family discussed how we each felt a call to serve God.

Because of our exhaustion, Bob Fitts, Jr.'s suggestion became more appealing. "Let's take the whole family to Hawaii," said Gary. "We'll check out YWAM and their University of the Nations campus in Kona. I think we need to rest. We'll see if God will reveal anything new to us."

It was the beginning of an incredible journey.

We arrived on the Big Island of Hawaii the first of September 1999, and stayed for one month. Part of the time we stayed in guest housing on this beautiful palm tree-covered University of the Nations campus located on a hill overlooking the vastness of the blue Pacific. The other portion of our stay was spent in a small, comfortable guesthouse owned by people affiliated with YWAM who generously allowed us to rent their (guest house) "ohana" for a very minimal fee.

Every morning was spent on campus. Justin and Nathan sat in on Discipleship Training School (DTS) classes for college-aged young people. The boys were getting really charged up about becoming missionaries. The other DTS students welcomed our sons as if they were part of the group.

Gary and I sat in on Crossroads DTS, which is for people 25 years or older, who had reached a crossroads in their lives and were seeking God for direction. We had never heard a speaker so zealous for God. God was calling us to proclaim the gospel to a needy world.

Campus worship services were Monday mornings and Wednesday evenings. The energy and enthusiasm of young people on fire for God was contagious. On Sundays we attended a church pastored by a YWAM leader. At mealtimes in the open-air "cafeteria," surrounded by the fragrant plumeria trees, we talked to students and staff to learn all we could about this place, which felt as if God's anointing rested on it.

Each afternoon we went to the beach, and I pondered all God was teaching me. As I relaxed in the warm sun, it felt as if I was resting in Jesus' arms. I grew stronger and more refreshed with each new day.

Life changed for our family. We would never be the same again. None of us felt we could return to living as we had before. Our hearts were turned to wanting to serve God.

We had to return home in October. It was impossible to explain to friends and relatives what had changed us. We were different somehow.

Gary and Justin returned to work. Nathan resumed his horticulture classes in college. I occupied most of my time playing my flute and teaching. A lot of time was spent seeking God for His will to be done in the lives of my husband, my sons and myself. But we were all experiencing a feeling of unrest. God's calling was there, we just didn't know when or how.

Justin was the first member of our family to make the bold step to give up his job and apply to the YWAM base in Kona, Hawaii. He left in January of 2000 for the three-month classroom lecture phase in DTS. Their team then went on a two-month outreach to Japan and the Philippines. Upon his return we could tell Justin was changed. He was passionate about helping start a college group at a new church he began attending. The pastor was excited at first, but his enthusiasm waned as

Justin's passion for people to come to know the Lord intimately became apparent. After a few short months, the pastor came to Justin and said, "You're just too zealous. It could scare new believers away." Justin began attending Campus Crusade for Christ and they were very happy to have a zealous young man join them. He rose quickly into leadership.

Three months later Nathan left for the U of N Kona campus where he enrolled in a course about permanent sustainable agriculture. Following the course, his team went to the Philippines and lived at an orphanage for two months installing a water catchment system, gardens, irrigation ditches and a fish pond.

Nathan phoned us from the Philippines. Even though there was static on the line we could hear the excitement in his voice. "I know now God has called me into the mission field. I want to spend the rest of my life teaching people in developing nations about permanent sustainable agriculture while teaching them about Jesus. No one needs to go hungry or thirsty in this world, and everyone needs to learn of God's love."

We were next. Gary took a six-month leave of absence from the bank. In October of 2000, Gary and I followed in our sons' footsteps and began Crossroads Discipleship Training School. Justin was left to care for our large house and our 10-year-old dog, Tucker.

On the first day of class I couldn't believe we were really there as students. The auditorium filled with 80 other students all at the crossroads of their lives seeking God for direction. As the keyboard and guitar began worship music my throat tightened with emotion, and I couldn't even sing. It was so beautiful, I felt as if I was experiencing a little piece of heaven. Tears streamed down my face as I soaked in God's love.

I learned so much about God. Each week we had a different speaker who taught us about the Father heart of God, the character of God, how to seek God's face and how to hear God's voice. Nathan was scheduled to begin his DTS in January. What a season for our family!

CHAPTER THIRTEEN

ON GUARD

Above all else, guard your heart for it is the wellspring of life.
PSALM 4:23

One week during the lecture phase of our Crossroads Discipleship Training School (CDTS) the speaker challenged us by asking, "Is there anyone in your life that you couldn't welcome if they walked through that door right now? Could you tell them you were glad they were here?"

Those questions hit me hard. Nathan's case was dismissed a year and a half ago, but I still didn't hold forgiveness in my heart. If Lisa Smith's family came through the doors of our classroom, I would want to lash out at them—to tell them about my pain. The ache within me was like a fresh wound whenever I thought about all we had been through. I wanted to tell Nathan's accusers what their actions cost us financially and emotionally. *Did they know Nathan lost his job, dropped out of college for a quarter and changed his major?* I fumed.

My head said it was wrong not to forgive, but my heart didn't want to let it go. Nathan had been wronged. A debt was owed, and it affected our whole family. At the very least we deserved financial reimbursement and an apology. I wanted to hold those who wronged us accountable. I wanted to see justice served.

Inside, I knew I was not being obedient to God's will. There was a deep groaning in my spirit as I wrestled with this decision. Two hours later I was still crying when I went to find Nathan. He was working on a backhoe in front of the dorms. He quickly got off when he saw me coming.

I told him what our speaker had said. "Nathan, we were all hurt. Most of all, though, you were hurt. Your character, morals and integrity were challenged. How can I forgive someone who hurt you like that?"

"Mom," Nathan said gently, as he looked directly into my eyes and laid his large, grass-stained hand on my shoulder. "Look where we are. Our whole family is serving God. We wouldn't be where we are unless we experienced all the crises we've been through in the last 10 years."

My heart began to soften. I gave Nathan a big hug. What Satan intended for evil, I trusted that God had changed to good.

"If you can forgive those who hurt you, then I need to forgive them, too."

I spent the afternoon praying and reading God's Word. My emotions needed to be directed in the right way. Sometimes when my feelings were repressed they built up like a volcano of resentment and bitterness exploding at unexpected times and on undeserving people. Such thoughts and actions do not bring glory to God, and I wanted to glorify God. I had to relinquish my right to anger and restitution. I had to decide if I was going to deal with my feelings in a way that is characteristic of God.

Forgiveness was necessary to set Nathan's accuser and myself free. After wrestling with it a while longer I found Psalm 32:1-5:

Blessed is he whose transgressions are forgiven, whose sins are covered. Blessed is the man whose sin the Lord does not count against him and in whose spirit is no deceit. When I kept silent, my bones wasted away through my groaning all day long. For day and night your hand was heavy upon me; my strength was sapped as in the heart of the summer. I acknowledged my sin to you and did not cover up my iniquity. I said, "I will confess my transgressions to the Lord"—and you forgave the guilt of my sin.

Harboring this resentment had weighed heavily upon me, and my strength was sapped. I prayed that Psalm as if I wrote it, then added, "God help change my heart. I choose to obey you."

The Holy Spirit helped change my heart, and I grew to have a passionate love of God and an intense hatred of the enemy. I truly forgave the girl who had falsely accused Nathan. Forgiveness followed an act of the will and obedience to God.

Years earlier I had attended a women's conference where I learned that in Biblical times if one person wronged another, an official paper was drawn up and posted in a public place. The debtor then became a bond slave to the person they had wronged. They could be held to their commitment or a kind master could choose to forgive the wrong, rip up the paper and set the bond slave free. At the conference we were encouraged to forgive those who had hurt us. We were asked to write the name of anyone who hurt us on a piece of paper and describe the pain they caused us. We then ripped up the "bond," burned it and set them free.

I set my bond slave free that day in Kona, and I was also released. Because God is my redeemer, I put all my frustration, bitterness and anger in His hands. I concluded that what I do with my feelings is a choice.

I remembered the stories of Samson and David, who were mighty warriors and administered justice. Each one, however, discovered their weakness, which turned to strength when they had faith to obey the Lord. In Nehemiah 6:9 he prayed to the Lord, *"Now strengthen my hands."* I prayed for strength spiritually, emotionally and physically.

Whenever I prayed that prayer I felt strength flowing back into me. Psalm 81:6 says, *"I removed the burden from their shoulders, their hands were set free."* Once I accepted the truth, the truth set me free like it says in John 8:32. The burden was being lifted from my shoulders.

My tears of anger and resentment turned to tears of joy. All I could do was praise God for what He had done for our family. Like the wall Nehemiah rebuilt around Jerusalem our family was being rebuilt stone by stone. The wall had become tall and strong. Gates were in place to keep the enemy out. We were restored.

A visiting pastor from Scotland prophesied over me in church before we left Washington. "Guard your heart to allow Me to work within you a new birthing process," he said as if God were speaking directly to me. I had no idea what it meant at that time, but the Lord brought me out of the darkness.

What does it mean to guard your heart? I wondered. I searched scriptures and commentaries, which revealed that to guard your heart means keeping both attitudes and emotions in balance. When the Bible talks about the heart it is referring to our personality. If I didn't guard my heart I could become hard-hearted and susceptible to the enemy's influence. If I guarded my heart against bitterness my eyes could stay focused on God. That takes authority away from the enemy. Guarding our hearts was a safeguard against fear, pride and unbelief. How I wish our family had learned this lesson before going through the last crisis.

I believe there was a great calling on the lives of each member of our family. We had the potential to rebuild the foundations of our family and become a stronghold for God. But we had to be wholly surrendered to God. Through devotion and obedience we would be setting up a guard that the enemy couldn't penetrate. If only our sons could have made choices to stand firm and unyielding in their faith when they were young it would have saved us all a lot of heartache.

"Thank you Heavenly Father for the cross and what it taught me. You called us to give You our all and all. Gary, Justin, Nathan and I will never be the same because we were challenged and changed. The light of Your love took the fear away."

I believe our family was chosen by God to follow Him in missions. I now have a greater understanding of why we had to go through many painful experiences…to be prepared and to glorify God.

Our lives are no longer our own. With healing in His hands He took our brokenness and molded us. He now guides the steps of our family, and I pray that through our ministry and our experiences God will continue to be glorified.

CHAPTER FOURTEEN

REBUILT

They will rebuild the ancient ruins and restore the places
long devastated, they will renew the ruined cities
that have been devastated for generations.

ISAIAH 61:4

The outreach phase of our Crossroads Discipleship Training School began in January, 2001. So much happened on outreach that it could be another book in itself. We witnessed miracles, and lives were transformed as a result of our team reaching out to a remote hill tribe. As outreach team leaders, Gary and I were chosen to direct our group for one month in Northern Thailand and one month on an island in the Philippines called Occidental Mindoro.

Before we left Gary prayed over the group, "Father God, break our hearts for the things that break your heart. Let us see through your eyes. Let us love what you love and hate what you hate."

God certainly answered that prayer. I learned to love the Thai people so much I didn't want to leave. Yet, my love for the Filipinos, in the small town of Mamburao, was at least as great as my love for our Thai friends. As the ferryboat pulled away and we waved good-bye to our hosts, my tears fell like raindrops into the South China Sea. Part of my heart would remain in each of those countries. I guess it's like the love you have for your children. When I had my first son I didn't think I could love another child like I loved Justin, but the moment Nathan was born I loved him just as much. There was plenty of love for both children. That must be the way God is. He has so much love there is more than enough for every one of us.

Gary and I returned from outreach to Bellevue, Washington, in April, 2001. When we walked into our home I'm sure the surprise showed on our faces. Gary's first words were, "Justin turned our house into a church."

Justin had become a leader in Campus Crusade for Christ at Bellevue Community College. A Bible study was meeting in our home and was growing larger each week. A band set up their stage in the solarium and my grandmother's antique marble top table was Justin's pulpit.

"We are visitors in a house that no longer feels like home," I replied laughing and feeling enormously blessed. Day and night young people filled our home. The band practiced a couple of nights a week, and the music was so loud we couldn't even hear each other talk.

Campus Crusade meetings were on Tuesdays, Generation Church met on Wednesday nights and leadership meetings were on Thursday nights. Sunday was called "marathon church." It began with church in the morning, the band started arriving in the afternoon to practice for the Bible study which opened with a pot luck dinner and went until midnight or later. God chose Justin to be a missionary right there in our home. We knew God was calling us elsewhere.

University of the Nations leaders phoned to ask if Gary and I would consider being on staff. Being "on staff" at a university sounds official, but in YWAM it actually means "volunteer." No one within the mission organization is paid—not the Chancellor, the CFO or the person who mows the lawn. Like missionaries in Africa or India, we would still have to raise our own support. It was a huge step from having two incomes to becoming missionaries and depending on others for support.

After praying about it we sensed God was telling us, "I have a wonderful adventure ahead for you. Trust Me."

I received confirmation when I read Jeremiah 29:11:

For I know the plans I have for you, declares the Lord, plans to prosper you and not to harm you, plans to give you a hope and a future. Then you will call upon me and come and pray to me, and I will listen to you. You will seek me and find me when you seek me with all your heart. I will be found by you.

Gary asked the bank for an early retirement package and was denied. He tried several angles to no avail. Even though there would be no retirement income until Gary turned 62 in twelve years, we knew beyond a shadow of a doubt that God had an assignment for us, so we accepted the U of N position.

This was a real leap of faith. I felt like Indiana Jones in *The Temple of Doom* movie when he stepped into the abyss out of faith and a stone appeared under his foot to support him. As Indiana Jones took another step, another rock came out of nowhere until he made it safely to the other side. If God were calling us He would support us as we made that step of faith.

We said goodbye to Justin, friends, relatives and, our old dog Tucker on July 4, 2001. I cried all the way to Hawaii on the plane, but the greeting we received when we arrived made us feel like royalty. Nathan and his fiancée Bethany were among the crowd that day in Kona welcoming us when we arrived with all our possessions in four large Rubbermaid tubs.

Nathan had fallen in love with Bethany at the U of N the first time we came to Kona in 1999. They were quickly serious about their relationship, but couldn't coordinate overseas missions trips. While Bethany was taking the Community Health Development School, Nathan was in the Philippines. Bethany was in Thailand while Nathan was on campus. Soon after we returned to Kona, Bethany left for an internship in Cambodia. She and Nathan decided that the only solution to this separation problem was to begin planning a wedding. A date was set for January 26, 2002, in Indiana.

We saw Nathan daily, and Justin called weekly. One evening in September Justin called and asked us to join him in praying that God would provide him with a wife. He was lonely. Justin had a lot going for him: His passion for the Lord was growing. He had a good job as a cashier at an up-scale grocery store and made good money. And he worked hard at keeping in shape, even winning body-builder competitions. What woman wouldn't want this big, strong, good-looking, Christian guy? But Justin had not been successful with girls on a long-term basis. The head injury seemed to scare them off.

Abstract concepts such as humor were hard for him to grasp. His frustration level was always right at the surface sparking occasional bursts of anger. These are all common symptoms of closed-head injuries, but challenging to Justin and those living with him.

One day Justin said to me, "I don't understand why I can't find a wife…I can do the three C's."

"What are the three C's?" I asked.

"I can cook, clean and cuddle," he said playfully.

I promised Justin to join him in praying for a wife. Surely there is a woman who would love a guy who had a decent job and could do the three C's. I had prayed for good wives for both my sons over the years so I determined to pray more intensely for Justin until just the right woman came along.

"Thank you God. Thank you God. Thank you God," were the first words out of my mouth as I woke up on January 26, 2002. The smell

of fresh coffee wafted up from the dining room of the bed and breakfast in Bloomfield, Indiana, where we were staying. I pulled the down
comforter up around my chin as tears of joy streamed down my cheeks.
It was Nathan's wedding day.

Months before Nathan and Bethany's wedding I determined that
I wasn't going to be a blubbering mother of the groom. That would be
a challenge since it didn't take much to make me cry—beautiful music,
pictures of loved ones, even Hallmark commercials. *If I cry my make-
up will run, and I'll look awful in the wedding pictures*, I thought. With
a picture of a stoic Queen Elizabeth firmly etched in my mind, I practiced my most dignified look. Nathan and Bethany had asked me to
play my flute at their wedding. If my throat was tight from crying I
wouldn't be able to play well. With their picture in front of me I practiced many hours. During the wedding rehearsal my Queen Elizabeth
façade worked well. My best friends flew in for the wedding, and
together we played "The Lord's Prayer"—me on my flute and they on
cello and piano.

The wedding day dawned exceptionally warm and sunny for
Indiana in January. That day, though, my stoic Queen Elizabeth look
totally melted like the snow. The first rush of emotion came when
Nathan called.

"Hi Mom," he said in a cheery voice. "I'm not allowed at Bethany's
because there's some tradition about the groom not seeing the bride
until time for pictures just before the wedding. So, I'm coming over to
have breakfast and hang out with our family for the day."

Nathan's last day as our "little boy." The tears flowed again when
he walked in and wrapped his big arms around me. I cried all day. It
didn't matter what it was about. Some were tears of loss; most were
tears of joy. *I'm just so blessed*, I kept thinking as I wept.

Bethany is a beautiful Christian woman. God heaped grace upon
Nathan by giving him this amazing young lady as a wife. But because
I'm a flute player, I too feel blessed with a daughter-in-law who, among
other qualities and talents, is a gifted pianist.

Nathan and Bethany wanted some time to pray alone before people began arriving at the church and the photographer began a myriad of poses. When we walked into the church foyer the doors to the sanctuary were closed. I peeked through the doors. My son and his bride were kneeling before the altar praying together. What a beautiful sight! Yes, I was in tears again. As the doors were opened they turned to walk towards us. Bethany's veil was atop her soft red hair, which was pulled back into a pile of curls exposing large, green eyes that sparkled like emeralds. Nathan's tux hung straight on his tall thin frame. They were a very handsome couple, and it was a beautiful wedding.

When the day was over and Gary and I settled into that big bed under the comforter, I fell asleep as I had awoken—with tears streaming down my cheeks whispering, "Thank you God. Thank you God. Thank you God."

About six months after we returned to our life with YWAM in Kona, Hawaii, we got a surprise call from Justin one morning.

"The house is becoming too much for me," he said. "I can't keep up with the yard. The blackberries are taking over the flowerbeds. Maybe I could buy a condo."

"It sounds like the end of an era," Gary said. "Maybe it's time to sell the house."

That house held so many memories. I had hoped we could hang on to it as a place to go back to for family Christmases. But it had become an anchor holding us down. After more discussion and prayer I agreed that we should sell the house.

Gary called our neighbor to ask if he might be interested in buying it. He called back a few days later, and we agreed on a price. The deal would close by the end of August, which meant we had to go back to Bellevue to clean out 30 years of accumulated memories and mementoes.

To us, three weeks sounded like plenty of time to clean out our 2,700-sq. ft. home. We planned to fly back to Indiana afterward for a week with Nathan and Bethany, and then return to Kona.

The day we arrived in Washington we tackled the challenge of downsizing. Not using or even missing something for over a year became our standard for getting rid of each item. Gary was in charge of the garage and the heavy items. I began selling, giving away or throwing away everything in the house. Some of my grandmother's antiques went to our kids and my sisters. Other antiques were sold to dealers and friends. Then we started giving things away. What we couldn't give away we threw into a huge dumpster. There was a joy that came with getting rid of clutter that had become a burden. Amazingly, after just three weeks the house got emptied and cleaned, Justin moved and the loan on the purchase of his condo closed one hour before we closed the sale of our house. We left for Indiana the next morning.

Our week with Nathan and Bethany was a wonderful time of rest and reflection. So much had happened in such a short time—the big wedding in January, the death of our faithful dog Tucker in June, the sale of our house and Justin's purchase of a condominium in September. We knew God had his hand in each event. It was the end of a chapter in our lives. Eagerly we anticipated what God had in store for us next.

CHAPTER FIFTEEN

BACK TO LIFE

Can they bring the stones back to life from those heaps
of rubble—burned as they are?

NEHEMIAH 4:2

W hen my family was falling apart,
it would have been logical to focus my heart on the Bible's promises for
families, marriages and children. But when our family desperately
needed transformation, I was motivated to study the process the Old
Testament leader Nehemiah used in rebuilding Jerusalem and the walls
surrounding it. I analyzed how this wise leader went about reconstruction to see if it could work for a family. Nehemiah saw Jerusalem in a
"heap of rubble" just as I saw our family.

NEHEMIAH RESPONDED RIGHTLY TO DISASTER—1:3

The Jews who survived exile to Babylon had returned to Judea, but
were in great trouble and disgrace. The wall of Jerusalem was broken

down and its gates had been torched. After 10 years of trouble and disasters we were also broken down emotionally and spiritually.

Pain and suffering is part of the common human experience. Loved ones die, accidents happen, divorce tears families apart, disease destroys a perfectly healthy body. When crises occur we often ask tough questions like, "Why is this happening to me?" "Why now?" "What did I do?" or "Where is God when I need Him?" Many believers before us have faced injustices. Job lost everything; Daniel was thrown into the lion's den; Joseph was falsely accused and imprisoned, yet, none of these great men lost their faith.

Each one of us contributed to our family crisis, and with the Lord's help, each had a hand in the rebuilding process. Gary had let his work become an escape from our family problems. Overeating was my false comfort. Alcohol and drugs helped numb the pain for the boys. Instead of dealing with the pain we ended up being consumed by it. We were Christians, but we had responded in worldly ways. We hadn't yet learned the difference between living a Christian life and living victoriously in Christ.

From time to time, a pastor would preach, "God will shape your character as He allows you to go through crises." Pridefully, I thought my character was just fine. *Why does my character need to be shaped? How does crisis shape my character?*

Later I learned from our experiences that crises caused me to be more sympathetic with others facing difficult times. Brokenness melted my pride, which caused me to be more compassionate and authentic. I became teachable as I became desperate for God.

Telling a testimony is a little like hanging out dirty laundry. Gary was open to sharing our story. Justin didn't have any problems with me giving the account of his accident and the hardships Gary, Nathan and I experienced as a result of it. When I posed the question to Nathan, I said, "Some readers won't believe you were innocent when you were charged with a crime against a child. Or they may think we were blind to any wrongdoing on your part just because you're our son."

Nathan responded strongly, "I have nothing to hide. God knows I was innocent, and He's the one I'm accountable to." As a family, we made a decision that if our testimony could help others, we should tell how our family crawled out of a heap of rubble and was rebuilt, even when all appeared to be in ruins.

It is a testimony to the world when Christians endure truly difficult circumstances and continue to embrace God's will for their lives.

In Revelation 12:11 it says, "*They triumphed over him (the enemy) by the blood of the Lamb and by the word of their testimony.*" By the word of our testimony, I believe that the hearts of other families in crisis may be touched and they, too, might be victorious over the one who delights in destroying lives. By God's grace we rebuilt, just as Nehemiah did.

NEHEMIAH HUMBLED HIMSELF AND ASKED FORGIVENESS—1:5-7

I would love to say we saw each other through the eyes of grace, forgave each other and through a long-term commitment, our family was mended. But, that's not the way it happened. The Scott family did things the hard way.

We came to the brink of self-destruction before we finally humbled ourselves before God and each other. We asked forgiveness for the pain we had caused one another. God taught us to see through His eyes. His grace revealed how important our family really was. Now, we're very close, and I believe it's due to remembering how we nearly lost that relationship. Grief could have hardened our hearts and we could have become angry, bitter or depressed. But we chose to love.

Sin separates. Jesus was separated from His Father on the cross because of our sins. When we could not be honest with each other, sin separated our family.

It is only grace, mercy, forgiveness and love that unite...or reunite. God demonstrated unconditional love, showing us the way to love one another.

When we show grace and mercy we are saying, "I love you, forgive you, and accept you just as you are." Grace stems from love and forgiveness. When we embrace His forgiveness we can then extend it to others.

Bear with each other and forgive whatever grievances you may have against one another. Forgive as the Lord forgave you.

COLOSSIANS 3:13

NEHEMIAH GAVE PRACTICAL DIRECTION—3:3

Nehemiah directed the Jews to begin with basic tools, and set them to work. With these tools the people began by laying heavy beams, then putting the doors, bolts and bars in the gates.

The difficulties in our life forced us to take up tools to grow spiritually stronger. Our basic tools were the Word and prayer. We dove into the Word to hear from God and find solutions to our problems. In this process we saw the importance of our own words to build up or tear down. When I was told that our boys were using drugs, angry words poured out of my mouth—words of death not life. Words said in anger can take a long time to undo. It seems like it takes 10 positive things said to undo one hateful thing said in anger.

In prayer we asked God to help us see our sons as he sees them. That enabled us to love them unconditionally in spite of their sin, and to find ways to build them up rather than attack their character.

NEHEMIAH STOOD UP TO THE ENEMY'S TAUNTS—4:1

Sanballat from Samaria ridiculed the Jews and encouraged neighboring nations to do the same.

Sometimes friends saw us going through hard times and felt they had to comfort us. In a rush to provide answers some people were led to give us "advice." Their desperation to say *something* occasionally caused more harm than good. "Maybe there's sin in your life and God is punishing you or teaching you a lesson," said one well-meaning acquaintance. Another said, "Maybe there's someone in your life you have not forgiven so God is allowing these bad things to happen." When Justin was in a coma, fighting for his life, one person said, "Maybe God needs another angel." I didn't find that comforting. I don't think God is that needy, and we don't become angels anyhow.

I found it more helpful for friends to entertain Nathan, bring meals, offer to clean our house or just sit and grieve with us. What held us up the most in times of crises was our church and many people we didn't even know who were praying for us.

John 9:1-6 is the story about a blind man. The disciples asked Jesus if the blind man's or his parents' sin caused his blindness. Jesus told them that neither the man nor his parents sinned.

We didn't cause most of the bad things that happened to our family, like Justin's accident and other medical problems. Difficult things happen to believers and non-believers alike.

In many ways our 11-month legal battle on Nathan's behalf was the most difficult crisis we went through. It was one thing to face physical pain, but quite another to have our son's integrity and character attacked unjustly. Just as the Jews were ridiculed and insulted by their enemies, the enemy attempted to break me down by telling lies, ridiculing and insulting me. Sometimes I heard the enemy whispering lies in my head like, "*If only you had been a better mother you could have saved your family from so much grief. If only you had prayed more…*" The enemy did his best to get me down; but he drove me to my knees. When I listened more closely, I could almost hear the sound of angels' wings.

NEHEMIAH POSTED GUARD—4:22-23

The Samaritans became nervous when they saw the wall surrounding Jerusalem halfway completed, and they began to believe the Jews were actually going to succeed in rebuilding their fortress. The enemy tried to stop the progress, so Nehemiah posted guard day and night. He instructed the Jews to never remove their armor—not even at night or when they stopped for refreshment.

For the Jews opposition came, not just from neighboring nations, but also from the unseen enemy. It was true for us as well.

I do spiritual warfare by singing praise and worship songs about being victorious over the enemy. In the name of our Lord Jesus Christ I want to send any evil spirits fleeing that may be threatening to harm my family, my friends or me.

Do spiritual warfare in a way that fits your personality, but DO IT.

Be on guard against the enemy. We have a choice—don't let the evil one win. He only stops when Christians take authority over him in the name of the Lord Jesus Christ. Jesus gave us the ability to do all He did, and more. Our family had to learn to use the authority God gave us. Romans 16:19 says, *"Be excellent at what is good, be innocent of evil and the God of truth will soon crush Satan underneath your feet…"*

NEHEMIAH PRAYED FOR ALL TO HEAR—4:4

The enemy can't read our minds, so when we pray out loud the evil one knows in whom we put our trust. Like Nehemiah, speak out verbally against the enemy who is all around us. God has promised He will inhabit the surroundings where we dwell when we call upon His name.

Gary prays out loud. When he takes authority over the enemy his voice becomes very big. I have seen Gary take authority over a fire that threatened a home for girls in Thailand. The fire turned back on itself and burned out.

NEHEMIAH ENCOURAGED THE PEOPLE—4:14

I learned that when I sought God through prayer and through the Word He revealed Himself to me. Colossians 4:2 says, "*Don't be weary in prayer; keep at it; watch for God's answers and remember to be thankful when they come.*"

When Justin was in Children's Hospital the church youth group gave him a sweatshirt, which he wore a lot. It said, "*Be strong and courageous,*" Deuteronomy 31:6. The passage goes on to say, "*Do not be afraid or terrified because of them (the enemy) for the Lord your God goes with you; he will never leave you nor forsake you.*"

He can bring calm to the storms. Praise Him in all circumstances not for what happened but for who He is. Raising our eyes to Him gives us a new perspective.

We were encouraged as we saw that stone by stone our family was being rebuilt. Through the story of our family we offer inspiration, vision and encouragement to others who can't see through the rubble and all seems lost.

NEHEMIAH PERSEVERED—4:6

Nehemiah encouraged the people to keep working. It took a lot of perseverance for the Jews to rebuild Jerusalem and it took a lot of determination for us to rebuild our family, but it was the key to victory. Many times God tests our ability to allow Him to do His work.

Keep pursuing God through His Word and persevering faith. Galatians 6:9 says, "*And let us not get tired of doing what is right, for after a while we will reap a harvest of blessing if we don't get discouraged and give up.*"

James 1:2 encourages us to consider it pure joy whenever we face trials. Testing our faith develops perseverance so we will become mature and not lack wisdom. Verse 12 continues, "*Blessed is the man who per-*

severes under trials because when he has stood the test, he will receive the crown of life that God has promised to those who love Him."

Never give up. Keep on working—keep fighting for what is important.

Gary was Justin's BMX coach and convinced him he could accomplish anything, if he wanted it badly enough. "Don't stop until you have crossed over the finish line," was his advice to Justin. Sometimes the lead biker would let up just before the finish line as Justin flew past to the trophy awaiting him. The encouragement Justin received from his dad-coach spilled over into other areas of his life.

When Justin was critically injured Gary encouraged Justin to keep up the hard work to recovery. We believe it was Justin's "never let up until you're over the finish line" attitude that brought him further in his recovery than even the doctors hoped.

HE FOUGHT WEARINESS AND DISCOURAGEMENT—4:10

The strength of the Jewish people was giving out, and they believed there was just too much rubble to rebuild the wall.

Usually Gary was the one who held our family up spiritually. He was in the Word every day and His faith was strong. For a short period of time we had a role reversal. Gary became so discouraged when Nathan's case dragged on and on that it was hard for him to concentrate at work. Nathan's freedom and proving his innocence became all-consuming. His fear for Nathan's future was overwhelming him.

As time drew closer to the trial Nathan had trouble eating and sleeping. He, too, became almost non-functional. There was so much rubble neither one of them could see past the mess.

During hard times God gives extra portions of grace when we cast our cares on Him, as it says in Psalm 55:22. God gave me mountains of grace when I felt like I was holding both Gary and Nathan up.

I am a strong swimmer and often swim a mile or more in the open ocean for exercise. One day on the way back from my swim I saw four people headed for a buoy about one half mile out from shore. One man was trying to keep up with his friends, but they were oblivious to the fact that he was struggling. Many years ago I was a lifeguard, but still remember the correct techniques. I swam near the man and offered assistance. He obeyed my instructions so I simply held him up. As I breathed slowly with him his breathing slowed down. Seawater is so buoyant that I convinced him to allow it to hold him up. When he was sufficiently rested we swam back to shore together.

That's how I felt during the time before Nathan's scheduled trial. I was the one holding Gary and Nathan above water. Convincing them to relax and allow God to carry the weight was a daily task.

He gives strength to the weary and increases the power of the weak. Even the youths grow tired and weary and the young men stumble and fall; but those who hope in the Lord will renew their strength. They will soar on wings like eagles. They will run and not grow weary, they will walk and not be faint.

ISAIAH 40:31

NEHEMIAH BECAME ANGRY—5:6

Nehemiah became angry with the nobles and officials for attempting to extract taxes from the Jews who had nothing. Jesus also demonstrated righteous indignation when he saw vendors attempting to convince the Jews that their offering wasn't good enough for God. They turned the temple courtyard into a marketplace.

Anger needs to be directed and expressed correctly. What we do with our feelings, including anger, is a choice. God gave us the emotion of anger to arouse us against evil. He intended it as a means to defend ourselves and those we love against injustice and evil. Anger lets the offending person know how we feel so they can make things right.

Don't react—respond. If we are reacting it is usually out of fear. We are acting out of love when we are responding. Responses are mature actions to difficult circumstances. If anger is uncontrolled it is destructive, and that does not bring glory to God.

Anger management had been a problem in our household. Gary sometimes demonstrated misdirected anger. If repressed, the anger built up like a volcano until it erupted. Often it was something at work that caused it, but he didn't explode until he got home. Dealing with anger was also Justin's greatest challenge. After his accident, frustration over lingering results of his head injury often spilled on the family.

The Holy Spirit will help us recognize whether our anger is against evil or our ego is getting in the way.

Deal with anger—use Jesus' character as a role model. It was appropriate to become angry when the temple was defiled. At other times, like when the Roman guards were nailing Jesus to the cross He demonstrated compassion, asking the Father to forgive them.

NEHEMIAH REPRIMANDED THE PEOPLE—5:9

Nehemiah told the officials that what they were doing was not right. He told them to walk in fear of God.

Even though we believed in God and His Word, when the stress became too great we did not behave in a way that glorified God. The twelve-step program teaches that a person is in a weakened state if they are hungry, angry, lonely or tired (HALT). Mostly we were tired and unable to cope.

NEHEMIAH WAS NOT DISTRACTED—6:1-3

Nehemiah did not stop rebuilding even when he knew the enemy was scheming to stop the process and harm him.

The spiritual enemy is capable of distracting us from faith in God. Until we get back into a quiet mood before God, our faith in Him may diminish and our confidence in the flesh can distract our mind. It is extraordinary what power there is in simple things that distract our attention from God. Refuse to be overwhelmed with the cares of this life.

Another thing that distracts us is the need for vindication. I sometimes find myself saying, "I must explain myself; I want people to understand." God gave us discernment and if we obey Him, we don't owe any explanations.

NEHEMIAH HELPED THE PEOPLE OVERCOME THEIR FEARS—6:9

The enemy was trying to intimidate the Jews and he tried to intimidate us.

A lot of people fear the dark, loss of employment, lack of money or any number of things. Children often fear the water or they're afraid to speak in front of their classmates. When I was young I was afraid of everything. As a mother I feared the loss of any member of my family. Especially when Justin was critically head-injured, I had to totally trust God and put Justin in His hands. In Nathan's case I had to believe that even if our son went to prison—like Joseph in the Bible—God was going to work all things for His purposes. God used the accusation against Nathan to stop us from self-destructing, so I believed He would work this for good, too. The New International Version (NIV) of the Bible says, "do not fear" 46 times; "do not be afraid" 125 times; and "fear not" 139 times. It is a command from God, and it is a comfort to rest in Him.

We had to face head-on our fear of losing our family, our reputation and our home. Our sons seem to have been born without fear, but they too had to face fearful challenges—Justin faced the prospect that he might not recover. And Nathan faced the possibility of prison. We all triumphed over these fears because of our confidence in the One who says He will never leave us or forsake us.

In Exodus 20:20 Moses said to the people, *Do not be afraid, God has come to test you, so that the fear of God will be with you to keep you from sinning.*

Many times I found comfort in Isaiah 40:20: *You will be protected from the lash of the tongue, and need not fear when destruction comes.*

NEHEMIAH PRAYED REPEATEDLY—6:10

Nehemiah prayed that God would strengthen his hands. I prayed, "Oh Lord, strengthen my heart."

I don't know if prayers saved Justin's life. A lot of people have prayed for loved ones who still died. When Abraham asked God to spare his people, God changed His plans. If God hadn't answered our prayers it would not have changed my faith. Either way I know it would have been God's will, and I trust Him.

I believe we witnessed a miracle as Justin recovered. Each time I witness a work of God or a changed life, my faith is increased. Every time a prayer is answered it causes me to want to spend more time in prayer.

NEHEMIAH ACKNOWLEDGED THE SINS OF HIS PEOPLE—8:7-8

Nehemiah humbled himself before God on behalf of the Jewish people and confessed their sins. Later, the Levites instructed the people in the law. They read from the Book of the Law, making it clear and giving the meaning so that the people could understand.

God is a good King and is concerned about those who serve Him. Our King does not want to see us grieved. He wants to give us gifts, guard and protect us. When we use God's Word we are given tools to rebuild our fortress. We simply need to obey.

To be honest, when it came to the accusation against Nathan of molesting a child, I didn't know if I could trust the laws of man. I was frustrated that the prosecuting attorney didn't see through the flaws in the case and dismiss it in the beginning. The only thing I could do was put my trust in God, and truth did prevail. Nathan's favorite song was one we sang in church, which claimed that we have the power to stomp upon injustice. He could be heard singing that song for weeks after the case was dismissed.

There are both laws of God and laws of our land. Jesus said we are to obey both. Household rules apply to this category as well. Our teenagers spent several years in disobedience of our household laws. It was easy to think I was an outstanding example for others until I took a closer look. I'm no better than anyone else. In fact I've broken God's laws and man's laws.

There are people who follow His laws and still miss God. Then there are those who break all His laws and miss God. Of greatest concern are those who believe they miss God because they break His laws.

NEHEMIAH WAS FULL OF JOY—8:10

The Lord wants to have an intimate relationship with us. Gary and I had been raised as Christians, but didn't know what it meant to have a personal, intimate relationship with the Lord through trials. He revealed Himself to us in many different ways. Our eyes were opened through an angel named Bobbie (Chapter 1). I saw something in her that went beyond happiness, and I longed for that inner joy. I thought I had it. What I had was circumstantial happiness. But joy is eternal.

Choose to rejoice. *"Be joyful always; pray continually, give thanks in all circumstances, for this is God's will for you in Christ Jesus" (Thess.5:18-19).*

Pain and suffering were not part of God's plan for humanity. It broke His heart when sin entered the world. He is a loving Father who grieves with us during times of crises. *"For the joy set before him, He endured the agony of the cross"* (Hebrews 12:2). Rejoicing in our sufferings is not trying to avoid them or grit our teeth in quiet submission. I don't pretend they never existed. God calls us to rejoice in tribulation—not in spite of it—but because of it. When we were going through difficult times I tried to remember that Jesus came to bear our pain and restore our relationship with the Father. God doesn't want to teach us to be strong; He wants to be our strength.

NEHEMIAH INSTRUCTED THE PEOPLE TO BE STILL—8:11

One of the biggest weapons against the enemy is peace. In Psalm 23 it says that He sets a table before us in the presence of our enemy. Can you imagine how frustrated the enemy would be if he had an army ready to attack, and we sat down to a banquet?

Throughout the Bible, God encourages us to cast all our cares on Him, trust Him, rejoice in everything, be still, and be at peace. Spiritual maturity is apparent when we have peace in the midst of the battlefield.

HE LED THE PEOPLE TO GIVE THANKS—8:6 AND 9:5-6

We, too, gave thanks to the Lord for He created all things and He remains faithful. I am still so thankful for all He has done for my family. As I wrote this book and had to relive each crisis we went through, I continue to be amazed at where we were and how far God has taken us in just five years.

NEHEMIAH'S HEART WAS AS FAITHFUL AS ABRAM'S—9:7

When crisis hit our family the church body surrounded us, and we were strengthened. It was the faith of others that held us up, prayed and took care of our needs. They carried us through hard times. Now we try to pass that love along when we see crises hit others.

If we learn how to walk through the hard times with God, He has promised to never leave us or forsake us (Deuteronomy 31:6), no matter how bad the circumstance. As I reached out to Him, He responded with comfort and hope.

Now when difficulties arise Gary has a favorite saying, "It's not the circumstance that counts, but who we are in the midst of circumstances. More importantly, where we see God living, moving and having His being in the midst of our circumstances is what matters most."

For Christmas of 1999 Gary made Justin, Nathan and me a very special gift. We each received a book called *The Scott Family Creed.* There is a section for favorite family scriptures that helped us through difficulties. "The Lord's Prayer" is one part, which includes an explanation of each phrase. One part was labeled "The Scott Family Theme," which is "Whatever you do, do it for the glory of God." That is my life's goal.

Billy Graham spoke to grieving families after the Oklahoma City bombing, which occurred on April 19, 1995. He comforted them then added, "Times like this will do one of two things; they will either make us hard and bitter and angry at God or they will make us tender and open and help us reach out in trust and faith… I pray that you will not let bitterness and poison creep into your souls, but you will turn in faith and trust in God even if we cannot understand. It is better to face something like this *with* God than without Him."

UNDER HIS WING

He will save you from the fowler's snare and
from the deadly pestilence. He will cover you with His feathers,
and under His wing you will find refuge.

PSALM 91:3-4

How can suffering or sorrow be right? What do I say when people ask, "How can God let bad things happen to good people like your family?" Believers and nonbelievers alike ask the "why" question.

"We live in a fallen world," doesn't seem to help many people. Why do some families experience far more tragedy than others?

Why? My answer is usually "I don't know." Or, "Because He is God and I am not." The more important question is, "How will I reflect God's character in the midst of crisis?"

Through each crisis, we were refined and made stronger like pottery that has withstood fire in the kiln. Everything God does is right, accurate and appropriate. He is sovereign and just. Nothing is a surprise to God. I want His character to be my character.

Our story may seem to contradict God's justice. Without hardships, I wouldn't have learned what I know to be true about God today. It was during weak times that I learned the most about God, especially that He has a purpose for everything.

God does not love a member of our personal family more or less than anyone else's.

I have prayed for physical healing, and I've had many people pray for me. While at a church service a number of years ago, the guest speaker asked people to come forward if they needed physical healing. That night I said, "Why would I ever turn down prayer?" But then, I have other issues to deal with when I don't get the result I want. I'm disappointed when others receive miracles and I don't. One day I felt God was telling me, "You are seeking healing, but you need to seek The Healer. Your healing won't come from someone else. It will come only from Me, and I want you to depend on Me."

I asked God, "*How have you been just to me and my family?*" He showed me a justice scale. One bowl was filled with my weaknesses. The other bowl was filled with my blessings and they were balanced. In spite of my shortcomings He has blessed me with two sons and a husband who are serving God with all their hearts.

Justin has grown into a strong man of God. He would like to be married but lives a happy and fulfilled independent life. Besides being a journeyman meat cutter, Justin ushers every Sunday and is very involved in a young professionals group at his church.

Nathan and Bethany continue to serve as full time missionaries in Thailand. They have given their lives to serve God and help people who can benefit from their skills in horticulture and health care.

Then God showed me my husband, Gary. I don't know anyone with more integrity than Gary. He's been a great father, provider and godly head of the household. Gary is a wonderful example to our family. Together, we were dependent upon God while raising our sons.

Gary and I are full-time missionaries and travel extensively. Disabilities don't stop me. I am extremely thankful that God called us to serve Him through Youth With a Mission.

Born with hip dysplasia, I was given a handicap to keep me in constant touch with my limitations. Now I take my limitations in stride because the weaker I get physically, the stronger I become in Christ.

I have gotten more disabled with age. Surgery on my cervical spine involved removing three bulging discs and replacing them with metal cages. Recently, I was told the prosthesis in my left hip is loosening, and I will need a revision again in a few years. That wasn't the news I wanted to hear, but God has used it for His glory when I share my story to help others.

God gave us His Word to answer our questions. Nehemiah saw what no one else could see. He knew that even though Jerusalem lay in a heap of rubble it could be rebuilt, stone by stone. That book encouraged me more than any other book in the Bible when I thought all was lost. Now our family's walls no longer lay in ruins.

In many ways our story also reads like the book of Job. I learned much from that book as well. Job 5:22 says, *"You will laugh at destruction and famine and need not fear the beasts of the earth."*

The book of Job is filled with "why" questions, but not a lot of answers. God gave us the book of Job so we could process grief and come through it as Job did—with a stronger faith and a humble spirit. Job's wife encouraged him to commit suicide and his friends offered ignorant suggestions. God did not answer Job's questions. Instead, He asked more questions:

Where were you when I laid the earth's foundation? Tell me, if you understand. Who marked off its dimensions? Surely you know! Who stretched a measuring line across it?

JOB 38:4-5

God goes on with more than 70 questions. Eventually, Job kneels as he comes to understand how big God is and declares, *"I am unworthy—how can I reply to you? I put my hand over my mouth,"* (Job 40:4). We need to be like Job and put our hand over our mouth to do more listening.

"My ears had heard of you, but now my eyes have seen you," Job finally declared (42:5). He realizes the question is not "why" but "whom." God was much more powerful than he ever imagined.

We have a choice: will we respond with despair or will we respond in faith like Job? We can cry, be frustrated, express righteous indignation and in the end, put a hand over our mouth.

Living without answers humbles us. We are not God. We do not know everything, nor has God promised to reveal all His reasons to us. As painful as it is, we simply need to trust Him. Once we let go of our demand for answers, we are liberated. We are set free to seek God for comfort, hope and healing.

God speaks to me during times of pain more than any other time. He also gives us comforting scriptures to turn to during those times about our promises of heaven and eternal life.

Hard times will either cause us to become hard and bitter at God, or they will make us tender and open to help teach trust and faith. Trust God, even if you cannot understand. It is better to face crisis with God than without Him.

When people ask Gary and I **why**, we can tell them **who**. That's what they really need, and that's a question we **can** answer.

Gary, Bethany, Nathan, Barbara and Justin